SOCIAL SECURITY DISABILITY INSURANCE

POLICY OPTIONS AND REFORM PROPOSALS

LAWS AND PROGRAMS

Additional books in this series can be found on Nova's website under the Series tab.

Additional E-books in this series can be found on Nova's website under the E-book tab.

LAWS AND PROGRAMS

SOCIAL SECURITY DISABILITY INSURANCE

POLICY OPTIONS AND REFORM PROPOSALS

HARVEY DANIELS
EDITOR

New York

For permission to use material from this book please contact us:
Telephone 631-231-7269; Fax 631-231-8175
Web Site: http://www.novapublishers.com

Library of Congress Cataloging-in-Publication Data

ISBN: 978-1-62948-776-2

Published by Nova Science Publishers, Inc. † New York

Contents

PREFACE

This book provides an overview of reform proposals designed to mitigate the growth in SSDI rolls. Most of the proposals discussed in this book focus on reducing the inflow (incidence) of new beneficiaries into the program. The authors also focus on information on two components of federal disability benefits, those provided through the Social Security Disability Insurance (SSDI) and the Supplemental Security Income (SSI) programs, policy options for the social security disability insurance program and provide a testimony of David C. Stapleton on securing the future of the social security disability program.

Chapter 1 – Social Security Disability Insurance (SSDI) program provides benefits to insured workers with disabilities under the full retirement age and their dependents based on an individual worker's earnings and work history in covered employment. Recently, some Members of Congress and the public have expressed concern over the financial sustainability of the SSDI program. Between 1980 and 2011, the number of disabled-worker beneficiaries grew 196.6%, whereas the number of workers insured for disability increased 50.9%. This increase in the ratio of disabled-worker beneficiaries to insured workers, or prevalence rate, has placed pressure on the Disability Insurance (DI) trust fund, which the Social Security Board of Trustees projects will be exhausted in 2016. Some of the increase in the SSDI prevalence rate stems from changes in the demographic characteristics of the insured-worker population. According to the Social Security Board of Trustees, the aging of the baby boom generation and a sharp rise in the number and incidence rate of female insured workers helped to propel the prevalence rate upward between 1980 and 2011. However, other factors may have also contributed to the growth in SSDI rolls. For example, instances of high unemployment and the increasing relative value of SSDI benefits to low-income workers may have induced more individuals to apply to the program. In addition, inconsistency in the determination and adjudication process might have increased the likelihood of denied claimants being awarded SSDI on appeal. Moreover, changes to federal policy that relaxed certain program eligibility criteria and increased the value of disability benefits relative to retirement benefits may have played a role in increasing the SSDI prevalence rate. To assist lawmakers in addressing the sustainability of the program, this report provides an overview of reform proposals designed to mitigate the growth in SSDI rolls. Most of the proposals discussed in this report focus on reducing the inflow (incidence) of new beneficiaries into the program. These proposals include implementing stricter SSDI eligibility criteria, improving consistency in the disability determination and adjudication process, and incentivizing employers to provide supported-work services for employees following the onset of disability (i.e., rehabilitation, workplace accommodation, and a partial wage replacement). On the other hand, some of the proposals seek to increase the outflow (termination) of beneficiaries from the program. Proposals to reduce the current beneficiary population entail providing stronger incentives for beneficiaries with some residual functional capacity to return to the labor force, as well as increasing the number of continuing disability reviews (CDR) performed by the Social Security Administration (SSA).

Chapter 2 – In general, the goal of disability insurance is to replace a portion of a worker's income should illness or disability prevent him or her from working. Individuals may receive disability benefits from either federal or state governments, or from private insurers. This report presents information on two components of federal disability benefits, those provided through the Social Security Disability Insurance (SSDI) and the Supplemental Security Income (SSI) programs. The SSDI program is an insurance program that provides benefits to individuals who have paid into the system and meet certain minimum work requirements. In contrast, the SSI program is a means-tested program that does not have work or contribution requirements, but restricts benefits to those who meet asset and resource limitations. The SSDI program was enacted in 1956 and provides benefits to insured disabled workers under the full retirement age (and to their spouses, surviving disabled spouses, and children) in amounts related to the disabled worker's former earnings in covered employment. The SSI program, which went into effect in 1974, is a needs-based program that provides a flat cash benefit assuring a minimum cash income to aged, blind, and disabled individuals who have very limited income and assets. To receive disability benefits under either program, individuals must meet strict medical requirements. For both SSDI and SSI disability benefits, "disability" is defined as the inability to engage in substantial gainful activity (SGA) by reason of a medically determinable physical or mental impairment expected to result in death or last at least 12 months. Generally, the worker must be unable to do any kind of work that exists in the national economy, taking into account age, education, and work experience. Both programs are administered through the Social Security Administration (SSA) and therefore have similar application and disability determination processes. Although SSDI and SSI are federal programs, both federal and state offices are used to determine eligibility for disability benefits. SSA determines whether someone is disabled according to a five-step process, called the sequential evaluation process, where SSA is required to look at all of the pertinent facts of a particular case. Current work activity, severity of impairment, and vocational factors are assessed in that order. An applicant may be denied benefits at any step in the sequential process even if the applicant may meet a later criterion. The SSDI program is primarily funded through Social Security payroll tax revenue, portions of which are credited to a Disability Insurance (DI) trust fund. In contrast, the SSI program is funded through appropriations from general revenues.

Chapter 3 – The Social Security Disability Insurance (DI) program pays cash benefits to nonelderly adults (those younger than age 66) who are judged to be unable to perform "substantial" work because of a disability but who have worked in the past; the program also pays benefits to some of those adults' dependents. In 2011, the DI program provided benefits to 8.3 million disabled workers, nearly sixfold the 1.4 million disabled workers who received benefits in 1970. Including the dependent spouses and children of those workers further increases the number of people receiving support in 2011 to 10.3 million. The growth in the program can be attributed to changes in multiple factors, including demographics, the labor force, federal policy, opportunities for work, and compensation (earnings and benefits) during employment. Over the past 40 years, outlays for benefits from the DI program (adjusted for inflation) have grown by more than nine times. During that period, the average benefit received by disabled workers rose from about $560 per month to about $1,050 per month in 2010 dollars. (Other programs also support workers with disabilities; for example, DI beneficiaries receive Medicare benefits that cost the federal government on average more than 80 percent as much as their DI benefits.) By comparison with outlays, revenues dedicated to the program have increased nearly fivefold since 1970. The divergence between the program's spending and revenues has prompted concerns about its financial sustainability. In 2011, spending on benefits in the

DI program was $128 billion, or 0.86 percent of gross domestic product (GDP); by contrast, the program's revenues totaled about $94 billion, or 0.63 percent of GDP. In 2022, the program's spending and revenues will be roughly the same shares of economic output as in 2011, according to the Congressional Budget Office's (CBO's) estimates. By 2037, revenues as a percentage of GDP will be little changed, but spending as a share of output will have fallen slightly, as the proportion of the working-age population that is age 50 or older (and thus more likely to receive DI benefits) declines. In this study, CBO in conjunction with the staff of the Joint Committee on Taxation (JCT) has estimated the budgetary effects of a variety of potential modifications to the DI program. In CBO's and JCT's estimation, two policy options that would alter the taxes that support the program would result in higher revenues of $13 billion or $28 billion in 2022. Seven policy options that would modify benefits could lead to declines in the rate of growth of the number of participants in the program and to cuts in the program's spending relative to CBO's currently published estimates; cuts in spending could range between about $1 billion and about $22 billion in 2022. In addition, CBO estimated the longer-run effects of each option relative to the agency's current long-term estimates: By 2037, the two revenue options would increase DI tax receipts in that year by 8 percent or 22 percent, and the seven spending options would reduce DI outlays by between 2 percent and 14 percent. Modifications to the DI program would necessarily affect several other federal programs, including, most significantly, the Social Security Old-Age and Survivors Insurance (OASI) program, Medicare, the Supplemental Security Income (SSI) program, and Medicaid. However, analysis of those interactions was outside the scope of this report. Restoring the DI program to a sound budgetary position would require combinations of the policies examined here or other changes to the program. From the perspective of the overall federal budget, the increases in taxes and reductions in spending considered in this analysis would improve the fiscal outlook to varying degrees but would leave very large imbalances between total federal revenues and spending if current policies were continued in all other respects. Alternatively, lawmakers could choose to modify the DI program in ways that would provide greater support to certain DI beneficiaries and increase spending for the program. CBO examined two policy options of that sort. Those options would increase DI outlays by $8 billion or $16 billion in 2022 and by 5 percent or 6 percent by 2037. Policymakers could also alter the program in more fundamental ways. CBO reviewed proposals for several such changes, and this report summarizes the main themes among them. Modifications might include promoting disabled beneficiaries' return to work—for example, by moving to a partial disability system that related benefits to the degree of disability or, in the case of newly disabled workers, by focusing on rehabilitation and reemployment rather than the receipt of benefits. Many of those alternatives have been implemented in various European nations, in part to reduce spending on disability programs, and that experience may provide some insight into the options' potential effects. But the changes in policy that those countries have instituted generally have been in place for such a short time that their fiscal impact is uncertain. Overall, CBO concludes, such fundamental changes might help move the United States' DI program toward budgetary balance in the long run but are unlikely to provide sufficient immediate cost savings to resolve the program's near-term financial pressures.

Chapter 4 – Testimony of David C. Stapleton, Senior Fellow, Mathematica Policy Research. Hearing on "Securing the Future of the Social Security Disability Insurance Program", presented September 14, 2012 before the House Committee on Ways and Means, Subcommittee on Social Security.

In: Social Security Disability Insurance
Editor: Harvey Daniels
ISBN: 978-1-62948-776-2

Chapter 1

SOCIAL SECURITY DISABILITY INSURANCE (SSDI) REFORM: AN OVERVIEW OF PROPOSALS TO REDUCE THE GROWTH IN SSDI ROLLS*

William R. Morton

SUMMARY

Social Security Disability Insurance (SSDI) program provides benefits to insured workers with disabilities under the full retirement age and their dependents based on an individual worker's earnings and work history in covered employment. Recently, some Members of Congress and the public have expressed concern over the financial sustainability of the SSDI program. Between 1980 and 2011, the number of disabled-worker beneficiaries grew 196.6%, whereas the number of workers insured for disability increased 50.9%. This increase in the ratio of disabled-worker beneficiaries to insured workers, or prevalence rate, has placed pressure on the Disability Insurance (DI) trust fund, which the Social Security Board of Trustees projects will be exhausted in 2016.

Some of the increase in the SSDI prevalence rate stems from changes in the demographic characteristics of the insured-worker population. According to the Social Security Board of Trustees, the aging of the baby

---

* This is an edited, reformatted and augmented version of Congressional Research Service, Publication No. R43054, dated April 29, 2013.

boom generation and a sharp rise in the number and incidence rate of female insured workers helped to propel the prevalence rate upward between 1980 and 2011. However, other factors may have also contributed to the growth in SSDI rolls. For example, instances of high unemployment and the increasing relative value of SSDI benefits to low-income workers may have induced more individuals to apply to the program. In addition, inconsistency in the determination and adjudication process might have increased the likelihood of denied claimants being awarded SSDI on appeal. Moreover, changes to federal policy that relaxed certain program eligibility criteria and increased the value of disability benefits relative to retirement benefits may have played a role in increasing the SSDI prevalence rate.

To assist lawmakers in addressing the sustainability of the program, this report provides an overview of reform proposals designed to mitigate the growth in SSDI rolls. Most of the proposals discussed in this report focus on reducing the inflow (incidence) of new beneficiaries into the program. These proposals include implementing stricter SSDI eligibility criteria, improving consistency in the disability determination and adjudication process, and incentivizing employers to provide supported-work services for employees following the onset of disability (i.e., rehabilitation, workplace accommodation, and a partial wage replacement). On the other hand, some of the proposals seek to increase the outflow (termination) of beneficiaries from the program. Proposals to reduce the current beneficiary population entail providing stronger incentives for beneficiaries with some residual functional capacity to return to the labor force, as well as increasing the number of continuing disability reviews (CDR) performed by the Social Security Administration (SSA).

INTRODUCTION

Concern among some Members of Congress and the public over the financial sustainability of the Social Security Disability Insurance (SSDI) program has been growing.[1] Between 1980 and 2011, the number of disabled-worker beneficiaries in receipt of SSDI rose 196.6% (from approximately 2.9 million to nearly 8.6 million), whereas the number of workers insured in the event of disability increased 50.9% (from almost 100.5 million to more than 151.7 million).[2] This increase in the ratio of disabled-worker beneficiaries to insured workers, or prevalence rate, has placed pressure on the Disability Insurance (DI) trust fund, insofar as inflation-adjusted program expenditures have increased 205.5%, from $43.3 billion in 1980 to $132.3 billion in 2011.[3]

Under its intermediate-cost assumptions, the Social Security Board of Trustees estimates that the DI trust fund will be exhausted in 2016.[4]

To assist lawmakers in addressing the sustainability of the program, this report provides an overview of reform proposals designed to mitigate the growth in SSDI rolls. The report is divided into four sections. The first section provides a brief background on SSDI, including program eligibility criteria, benefits, and the determination and adjudication process. The second section discusses the growth in SSDI rolls since 1980 by examining historical entry and exit program trends. Drawing upon research from government agencies, academic researchers, and public policy organizations, the third section of the report investigates some of the potential factors behind the growth in the SSDI prevalence rate, including changes in the demographic and economic characteristics of the insured-worker population, inconsistency in the administration of the program, and legislative changes to federal policy. The fourth section of the report examines various reform proposals to abate the growth in SSDI rolls, namely, stricter eligibility criteria, improved program administration, stronger return-to-work incentives, and supported-work policies. Although this report discusses potential savings from certain reform proposals, it does not specifically examine the effects of the proposals on the solvency of the DI trust fund.[5]

BACKGROUND ON SSDI

Eligibility

Enacted in 1956 under Title II of the Social Security Act, SSDI is a form of social insurance designed to provide protection against the risk of economic loss from the inability to work due to a disabling condition or impairment. Administered by the Social Security Administration (SSA), SSDI provides benefits to insured workers with disabilities under the full retirement age and their dependents (spouses, widow[er]s, and children) based on an individual worker's earnings and work history in covered employment.[6] In general, 40 work credits (quarters of coverage) are required to qualify for SSDI, 20 of which were earned in the last 10 years ending with the year of disability onset.[7] However, individuals who become disabled before the age of 31 need fewer work credits to qualify for SSDI benefits.[8]

To satisfy the disability requirement, an insured worker must be unable to engage in any substantial gainful activity (SGA) by reason of any medically determinable physical or mental impairment that can be expected to result in death or that has lasted or can be expected to last for a continuous period of not less than 12 months.[9] For 2013, SSA defines SGA as monthly earnings above $1,740 for statutorily blind individuals and $1,040 for non-blind individuals.[10]

Benefits

Cash benefits are based on a worker's past average monthly earnings, indexed to reflect changes in national wage levels (up to five years of the worker's low earnings are excluded).[11] SSA annually adjusts benefit levels to account for inflation through Cost-of-Living Adjustments (COLA), as measured by the Consumer Price Index for Urban Wage Earners and Clerical Workers (CPI-W).[12] SSA may offset cash benefits if a disabled worker also receives workers' compensation or other public disability benefits.[13] New beneficiaries receive cash benefits after a five-month waiting period from the time of disability onset.[14] In March 2013, the average monthly cash benefit was $1,129.61 for a disabled worker, $302.75 for a spouse of a disabled worker, and $336.84 for a child of a disabled worker.[15]

In addition to cash benefits, disabled-worker beneficiaries also receive health care coverage under Medicare 24 months after program eligibility begins (29 months after the onset of disability).[16] Moreover, SSDI beneficiaries may also meet the eligibility requirements for Supplemental Security Income (SSI).[17] SSI is a needs-based program that provides cash benefits to ensure a minimum income to aged, blind, or disabled individuals with limited income and assets.[18] In 2011, nearly 1.4 million disabled workers and their dependents concurrently received SSDI and SSI cash benefits.[19]

Determination and Adjudication Process

To initiate the claims process for SSDI benefits, an insured worker must first file an application with SSA either through the agency's website or by making an appointment at a local SSA field office.[20] Applications that meet the work history and SGA requirements are then forwarded to a Disability Determination Service (DDS). DDSs, which are fully funded by the federal government, are state agencies tasked with making disability determinations based on national standards established by SSA. During the disability determination process, DDS examiners—with the help of medical and psychological consultants—evaluate a claimant's medical impairment against SSA's *Listing of Impairments*. If a claimant's impairment meets (or is of equal severity to) the criteria in the listings, SSA considers the claimant to be disabled and therefore eligible for SSDI. Claimants who do not meet the medical criteria in the listings proceed to a more individualized assessment that examines their residual functional capacity to perform either any past relevant work or other work that exists in the national economy. If a claimant cannot perform such work, SSA approves his or her application for SSDI.

If a claimant's application for SSDI benefits is denied at any point during the disability determination process, he or she has the right to appeal the decision.[21] During the appeals process, claimants may present additional evidence or arguments to support their case, as well as appoint a representative to act on their behalf.[22] The appeals process is composed of four stages: (1) reconsideration by a different examiner from the state DDS office, (2) a hearing before an Administrative Law Judge (ALJ), (3) a review before the Appeals Council, and (4) filing suit against SSA in U.S. district court.[23] At each stage of the appeals process, claimants or their representatives must request an appeal to the next level, in writing, within 60 days of receiving notice of the prior decision. On rare occasions, SSDI cases are appealed beyond U.S. district court to the U.S. court of appeals and, ultimately, the U.S. Supreme Court.

TRENDS IN THE SSDI PROGRAM SINCE 1980

Enrollment

Over the past 30 years, SSA experienced an increase in the number of SSDI applications submitted to its offices. Between 1980 and 2011, the annual number of disability applications grew 123.1% (from nearly 1.3 million to almost 2.9 million).[24] As Figure 1 illustrates, most of the growth in SSDI applications began in 2000. From 1980 to 1999, the annual number of applications received by SSA remained roughly constant, averaging about 1.1 million between 1980 and 1989, and 1.3 million from 1990 to 1999; however, between 2000 and 2009, the average annual number of applications for disability rose to more than 2.0 million.

As with applications, the number of awards for disability increased as well. Between 1980 and 2011, the annual number of SSDI awards granted by

SSA grew 137.9% (from over 420,300 to more than 1.0 million). However, unlike applications, awards increased at a somewhat steadier rate, averaging 408,300 between 1980 and 1989; 601,100 from 1990 to 1999; and 796,200 between 2000 and 2009. Awards as a percentage of applications for SSDI increased from 33.3% in 1980 to 52.0% in 1998, before declining to 35.4% in 2011.[25]

SSDI awards per 1,000 insured workers rose 58.1% during this period (from 4.3 in 1980 to 6.8 in 2011). Insured workers are individuals who meet the work-history requirements for disability benefits. The number of awards per 1,000 insured workers is a rough estimate of the enrollment (incidence) rate of disabled-worker beneficiaries in the SSDI program.[26]

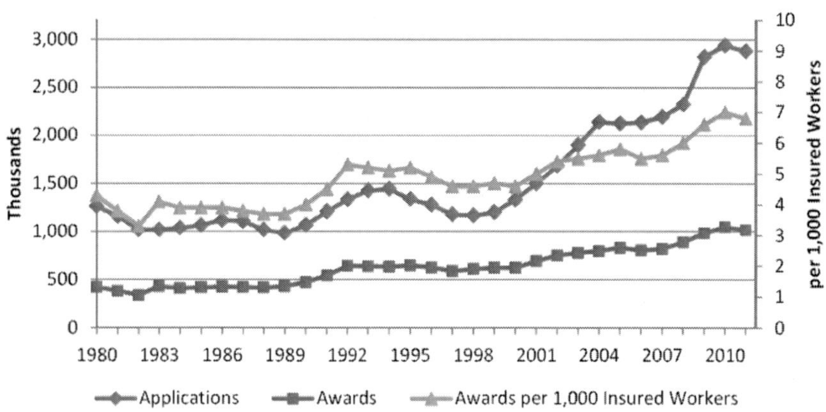

Source: Social Security Administration, *Annual Statistical Supplement to the Social Security Bulletin, 2012*, February 2013, Table 6.C7.

Notes: Applications and Awards are in thousands (left axis).The measure "awards per 1,000 insured workers" is in single digits (right axis). Insured workers are individuals who meet the work-history requirements for SSDI benefits.

Figure 1. SSDI Applications and Awards; 1980-2011.

Terminations

In general, SSA continues to pay benefits to SSDI recipients as long as they are disabled, ineligible for OASI retirement benefits, and have monthly earnings at or below the SGA threshold. However, when SSA determines that beneficiaries no longer meet SSDI's eligibility criteria, the agency will remove them from the program and terminate their cash and medical benefits.[27]

Although the overall number of disabled-worker terminations increased 44.4% between 1980 and 2009 (from 434,637 to 627,648), the ratio of disabled-worker terminations to insured workers (hereinafter "termination rate") actually decreased 45.3% (from 145.4 to 79.5 disabled-worker terminations per 1,000 insured workers).[28]

As depicted in Figure 2, three main factors drive the termination rate: death, conversion, and recovery. The beneficiary death rate decreased 40.2% between 1980 and 2009 (from 47.8 to nearly 28.6 disabled-worker terminations per 1,000 insured workers), reflecting the trend in the U.S. population of declining mortality rates across all age groups.[29] Between 1980 and 2009, the conversion rate fell 36.9% (from 68.1 to almost 43.0 disabled-worker terminations per 1,000 insured workers). A conversion termination occurs when SSA automatically converts a disabled-worker benefit to a retired-worker benefit under the Old-Age and Survivors Insurance (OASI) program due to a disabled worker reaching full retirement age (FRA). FRA is the age at which unreduced retirement benefits are first payable.[30] From 1980 to 2009, the recovery rate declined 79.6% (from 28.5 to about 5.8 disabled-worker terminations per 1,000 insured workers). Recovery refers to individuals removed from SSDI because they no longer meet SSA's definition of disability due either to a medical improvement or demonstrable ability to engage in SGA.

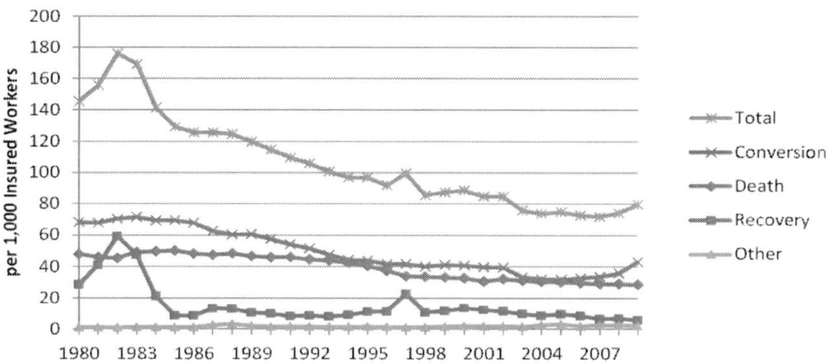

Source: Tim Zayatz, *Social Security Disability Insurance Program Workers Experience: Actuarial Study No. 114*, Social Security Administration, 1999, Table 5, and subsequent editions.

Notes: Data from 1980 to 1985 compiled from Actuarial Study No. 114, while data from 1986 to 2009 compiled from Actuarial Study No. 122.

Figure 2. SSDI Disabled-Worker Termination Rates; By Type (1980-2009).

The rise in the recovery rate during the early 1980s stemmed mainly from the enactment of the Social Security Disability Amendments of 1980 (P.L. 96-265), which expanded the use of continuing disability reviews (CDR) for all non-permanently disabled beneficiaries.[31] CDRs are periodic medical reevaluations to determine whether disabled beneficiaries continue to meet SSA's definition of disability.[32] A major review of the SSDI program after the passage of the 1980 amendments resulted in a significant increase in the recovery rate between 1980 and 1982.[33] However, the political backlash over the implementation of the reviews led to a 1983 temporary moratorium on CDRs for most mental impairment cases and an increase in the percentage of beneficiaries designated as permanently disabled and therefore subject to less frequent reviews.[34] Consequently, the recovery rate fell below its 1980 level.[35]

The 1997 increase in the recovery rate largely resulted from the passage of the Contract with America Advancement Act of 1996 (P.L. 104-121), which terminated the benefits of SSDI and SSI recipients whose drug addiction and alcoholism (DA&A) significantly contributed to their disability.[36] However, since DA&A beneficiaries represented only around 2.6% of all disabled adults on SSDI and SSI in 1996 and new applicants could no longer claim disability based on DA&A, P.L. 104-121's impact on the overall trend in the SSDI recovery rate was minimal.[37]

Starting in 2002, the recovery rate contracted again, in part because of a reduction in the number of medical CDRs performed by SSA. The Contract with America Advancement Act of 1996 authorized additional funds for CDRs but only for fiscal year (FY) 1996 through FY2002.[38] In FY2003, the additional funding for CDRs lapsed and SSA shifted its focus away from CDRs toward processing the growing number of initial disability claims.[39] As a result, the number of medical CDRs performed by SSA dropped from an all-time high of 876,802 in FY2000 to 207,637 in FY2007, before climbing back up to 443,233 in FY2012.[40]

Program Size

Between 1980 and 2011, the overall number of disabled-worker beneficiaries and their dependents increased 125.5% (from about 4.7 million to more than 10.6 million).[41] Most of the growth in the program stemmed from disabled-worker beneficiaries, whose ranks rose from around 2.9 million to almost 8.6 million—an increase of 196.6% (Figure 3). Conversely, the number of spouses of disabled workers on SSDI decreased 64.5% during this period (from almost 461,900 to more than 164,000). The number of children of disabled workers receiving benefits expanded rather modestly compared with disabled workers, increasing 35.7% (from nearly 1.4 million in 1980 to roughly 1.9 million in 2011).

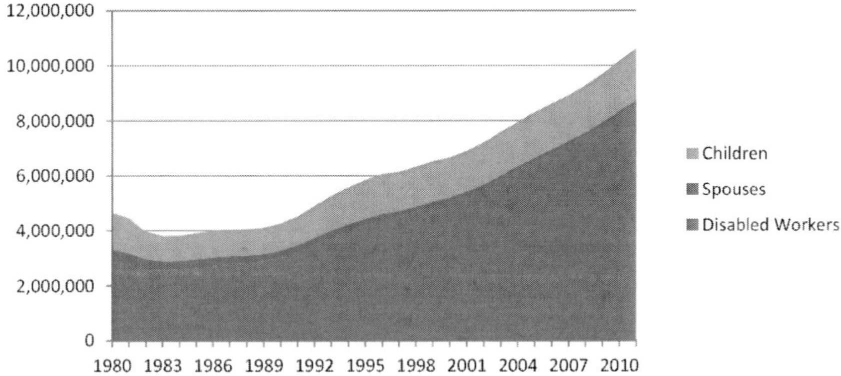

Source: Computed from the Social Security Administration, Annual Statistical Report on the Social Security Disability Insurance Program, 2011, Table 1, p. 17.

Notes: The category "Children" includes dependent children under the age of 18, dependent student children between the ages of 18 and 19, as well as disabled adult children of disabled workers. Disabled adult children can receive benefits at age 18 or older if they are unmarried and the disability began before age 22. To qualify for spousal benefits, the spouse of a disabled worker must either have a child under the age of 16 or a disabled child in his or her care or be at least 62 years of age. Disabled widow(er)s and disabled adult children of retired or deceased workers are not included in the graph above because payments for their benefits are made from the OASI trust fund.

Figure 3. SSDI Disabled-Worker Beneficiaries and Their Dependents; 1980-2011.

The size of the SSDI program is largely the function of two main factors: the incidence (enrollment) rate of beneficiaries in the program and the termination rate of beneficiaries from the program.[42] From 1980 to 2011, a marked rise in the incidence rate, coupled with a steady decline in the termination rate, resulted in an appreciable increase in the number of beneficiaries on SSDI. The prevalence rate measures the total number of disabled-worker beneficiaries relative to the overall insured-worker population in a given year. Between 1980 and 2011, the gross (unadjusted) prevalence rate grew 103.6% (from 28 to 57 disabled-worker beneficiaries per 1,000 insured workers; Figure 4).[43] With the increase in the gross prevalence rate, the fraction of the working-age resident population (aged 18-64) receiving SSDI benefits rose from 2.1% in 1980 to 4.6% in 2011.[44]

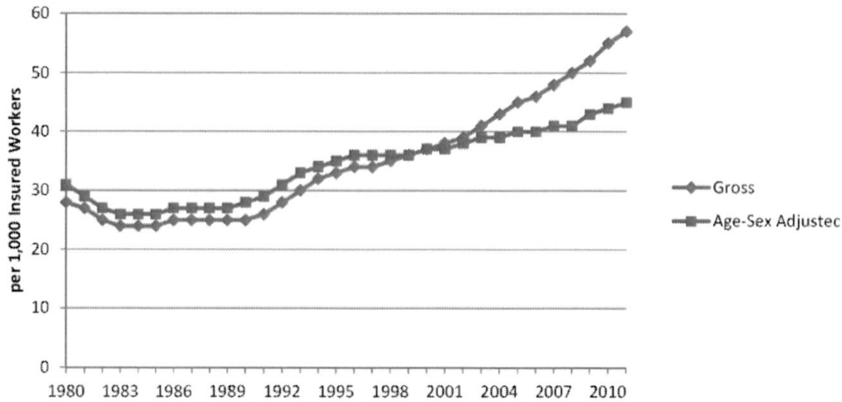

Source: The Social Security Board of Trustees, The 2012 Annual Report of the Board of Trustees of the Federal Old-Age and Survivors Insurance and Federal Disability Insurance Trust Funds, Table V.C5, p. 131.

Notes: The age-sex-adjusted rate is set to the age-sex distribution of the insured-worker population in the year 2000.

Figure 4. SSDI Disabled-Worker Prevalence Rates; 1980-2011.

When one adjusts the prevalence rate to control for the effects of changes in the age-sex distribution of the insured-worker population over time, the upward trend remains conspicuous, albeit somewhat less pronounced. Age-sex adjusting permits a more "meaningful comparison" over extended periods, insofar as it "isolates the changing trend in the true likelihood of receiving benefits for the insured population, without reflecting changes in the age distribution of the population."[45] From 1980 to 2011, the age-sex-adjusted prevalence rate grew 45.2% (from 31 to 45 disabled-worker beneficiaries per 1,000 insured workers).

Factors Behind the Growth in SSDI Rolls

Some disagree over the primary drivers behind the increase in the ratio of disabled-worker beneficiaries to insured workers. The growing gap between the gross and age-sex-adjusted prevalence rates suggests that changes in the age-sex distribution of the insured-worker population have contributed to the increase in the SSDI prevalence rate over time (Figure 4). However, the increase in the age-sex-adjusted prevalence rate indicates that the growth in SSDI rolls is not entirely attributable to changes in the age-sex distribution of the population. Changes in the economic incentives to apply for SSDI, inconsistency in the administration of the program, and legislative changes to federal policy may have also helped to increase the prevalence of SSDI receipt among the insured-worker population. This section examines some of the more salient explanations for the rise in SSDI rolls, as well as discusses other potential factors.

Changes in the Demographic Characteristics of Insured Workers

Part of the reason why SSDI rolls have expanded stems from the growth in the size of the insured-worker population.[46] Between 1980 and 2010, the U.S. working-age population (aged 18-64) increased 41.6% (from more than 137.2 million to almost 194.3 million), whereas the number of workers insured in the event of disability grew 49.8% (from nearly 100.5 million to around 150.5 million).[47] The combination of an increase in the number of insured workers due to population growth and a rise in the percentage of the working-age population insured for disability resulted in an expansion in the size of the insured-worker population.[48] In addition, the rise in the incidence of benefit receipt among the disability-exposed population has played a role in exacerbating the growth in SSDI rolls. From 1980 to 2009, the gross incidence (enrollment) rate grew 56.8% (from 4.4 to 6.9 awards per 1,000 disability-exposed workers).[49]

The following subsection investigates how changes in the demographic characteristics of the population may have increased both the size and incidence rate of the insured-worker population, thereby enlarging disability rolls.

Helpful Definitions

Insured-Worker Population: The total number of workers who meet the work-history requirements for disability benefits

Prevalence Rate: The ratio of the number of disabled-worker beneficiaries in current-payment status each year to the insured-worker population

Disability-Exposed Population: The total number of workers who meet insured requirements but are not yet receiving benefits

Incidence Rate: The ratio of the number of new beneficiaries awarded benefits each year to the disability-exposed population

A Sharp Rise in the Number and Incidence Rate of Female Insured Workers

The latter half of the 20th century witnessed a marked expansion of women in the labor force. Between 1950 and 1999, the labor force participation rate for women aged 16 and older nearly doubled (from 33.8% to an all-time high of 60.0%).[50] The higher participation rate afforded more women the opportunity to earn enough quarters of coverage to qualify for disability insurance. From 1980 to 2010, the number of female workers insured for disability rose 79.9% (from almost 40.2 million to more than 72.3 million).[51] Whereas the share of working-age men (aged 15-64) insured for disability declined during this period from 77% to 74%, the portion of working-age women insured for disability increased from 51% to 68%.[52]

The growth in the size of the female insured-worker population coincided with a rapid rise in the incidence rate of women in the SSDI program. Whereas the age-adjusted incidence rate for men entering the SSDI program increased 22.0% between 1986 and 2009 (from 5.0 to 6.1 awards per 1,000 disability-exposed male workers), the age-adjusted incidence rate for women rose 68.6% (from 3.5 to 5.9 awards per 1,000 disability-exposed female workers).[53] According to the Social Security Board of Trustees, the increase in the incidence of benefit receipt among female insured workers helped propel the age-sex-adjusted prevalence rate upward.[54] However, SSA's Chief Actuary projects that both male and female age-adjusted incidence rates should stabilize between five and six awards per 1,000 disability-exposed workers in the future.[55]

A Shift in the Age Distribution of Inured Workers

In addition to the rise in women's labor force participation, the aging of the large baby boom generation—individuals born between 1946 and 1964—also contributed to the increase in SSDI rolls.[56] Beginning in 1996, working-age baby boomers increasingly entered their most disability-prone years (aged 50 to full retirement age [FRA]), thereby shifting the age distribution of the insured-worker population from younger workers (aged 25 to 44) to older workers (aged 45 to FRA).[57]

The shift from younger to older insured workers helped to increase the gross incidence and prevalence rates, inasmuch as older workers have a higher likelihood of benefit receipt relative to younger workers.[58] In making a disability determination, DDS examiners take into account the claimant's medical condition, as well as vocational factors such as age, education, and work experience. Since eligibility criteria typically become less stringent with age, SSA is more likely to award benefits to older insured workers compared to younger workers.[59] Between 1986 and 2009, the portion of SSDI benefits awarded to younger insured workers (aged 25-44) decreased from 30.0% to 22.0%, whereas the share of benefits awarded to older workers (aged 45 to FRA) increased from 66.7% to 75.5%.[60] However, the Social Security Board of Trustees expects the gross prevalence rate to grow more slowly in the future as baby boomers increasingly become eligible for full OASI retirement benefits.[61]

Slightly Higher Work-Limiting Disability Rates

Changing trends in the health status of the U.S. population may have also helped to enlarge SSDI rolls. Over the past 40 years, advances in medical care and technology significantly reduced the death rate in the United States.[62] Between 1970 and 2010, the crude (unadjusted) mortality rate fell 15.4 % (from 945.3 to 799.5 deaths per 100,000 population).[63] When one controls for the effects of the aging U.S. population, the reduction in mortality is even more pronounced. From 1970 to 2010, the age-adjusted mortality rate declined 38.9% (from 1,222.6 to 747.0 deaths per 100,000 population).[64]

The decreased likelihood of dying in a given year helped to increase the chance of an individual surviving to his or her most disability-prone years (aged 50 to FRA). One study found that only 68% of males born in 1921 survived to the age of 60 compared with 78% of males born in 1941.[65] The increased likelihood of surviving to their most disability-prone years may have lowered the overall health of the insured-worker population, consequently raising the incidence of benefit receipt. According to data from the Current Population Survey (CPS), the share of men and women aged 21-64 reporting a work limitation due to a disability rose from 7.9% in 1981 to 8.5% in 2011.[66] However, some researchers contend that the health of individuals in their most disability-prone years has actually improved since 1980.[67] In fact, one study concluded that the improved health of individuals aged 50-64 might have slowed the growth in SSDI rolls between 1984 and 2002.[68]

Part of the problem in determining the trend in the prevalence of work-limiting disabilities in the U.S. population stems from the fact that there is no single, universally accepted definition or measure of disability.[69] Although many of the large demographic surveys used by researchers and the federal government specifically ask questions pertaining to work-limiting disabilities, the wording and complexity of the questions often differs. Moreover, because surveys are self-reporting, the definition of what constitutes a work-limiting disability often rests entirely on the subjectivity of the respondent. That said, given the relatively small increase in the CPS measured disability prevalence rate, it seems unlikely that the change in the prevalence of work-limiting disabilities in the U.S. population can adequately explain the growth in SSDI rolls.

Changes in the Economic Incentives to Apply for SSDI

The decision to apply for SSDI may be influenced not only by health status but also by economic opportunities. The relative value of SSDI cash and medical benefits may induce individuals with limited income and assets to apply to the program. Although the initial determination process screens out most non-meritorious claimants, SSA may grant awards to some claimants on the margin of program entry who could potentially work but choose not to due to economic circumstances. This subsection outlines how changes in the economic incentives to apply for SSDI may have increased the incidence of benefit receipt and thus expanded disability rolls.

A Rise in the Unemployment Rate

During periods of strong economic growth, individuals who qualify for SSDI might forgo applying for benefits and decide to seek or continue employment. However, when adverse shocks to the national economy reduce growth and increase unemployment, individuals who might otherwise choose to work may instead apply for SSDI benefits as a form of unemployment assistance. An extensive body of literature has empirically found a positive relationship between the unemployment rate and SSDI application rate.[70] With the exception of the period between 1980 and 1984, instances of high unemployment are associated with an increase in SSDI applications. As Figure 5 illustrates, the recent recession (December 2007 to June 2009) contributed to a conspicuous spike in the number of SSDI applications submitted to SSA; between 2007 and 2009, SSDI applications increased 27.3% (from almost 2.2 million to more than 2.8 million).[71]

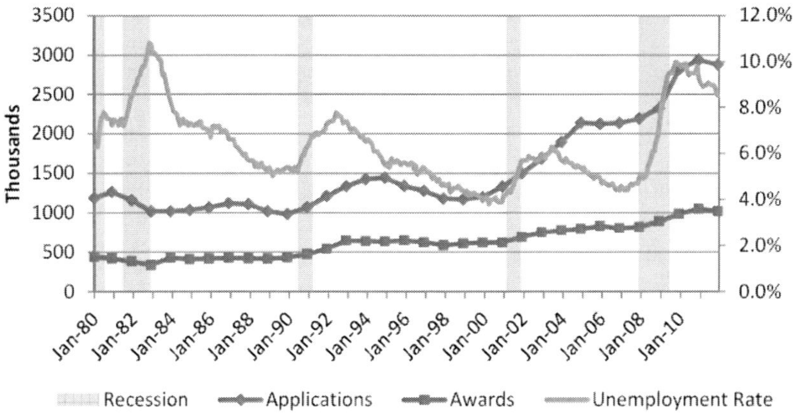

Source: Application and Award data compiled from the Social Security Administration, *Annual Statistical Supplement to the Social Security Bulletin, 2012*, February 2013, Table 6.C7. Unemployment data is from the Bureau of Labor Statistics (BLS). Recession data is from the National Bureau of Economic Research (NBER).

Notes: Applications and Awards are in thousands (left axis). The unemployment rate (right axis) is the number of all unemployed individuals aged 16 and older as a percentage of the civilian non-institutionalized labor force. BLS considers individuals to be unemployed if they do not have a job, have actively looked for work in the past four weeks, and are currently available for work. Shaded areas indicate a recession. NBER defines recession as a "significant decline in economic activity spread across the economy, lasting more than a few months, normally visible in real Gross Domestic Product (GDP), real income, employment, industrial production, and wholesale-retail sales."

Figure 5. SSDI Applications and Awards During Instances of High Unemployment; January 1980 – December 2011.

The relationship between the unemployment rate and the number of SSDI awards granted by SSA is somewhat more ambiguous, inasmuch as the award year may not coincide with the application year due to a prolonged determination or appeals process.[72] Moreover, one study found that a claimant's likelihood of receiving an award at the initial determination level decreases as the unemployment rate rises.[73] Nevertheless, the overall number of SSDI awards issued by SSA does appear to increase during instances of high unemployment, albeit to a lesser extent relative to the number of SSDI applications.[74] Between 2007 and 2009, the number of SSDI awards granted by SSA increased 20.3% (from 818,500 to 984,500).[75]

An Increase in the Relative Replacement Wage

In addition to changes in the business cycle, the value of cash benefits relative to potential earnings may also affect a worker's decision to apply for SSDI. Disability insurance protects workers against the risk of economic loss from the inability to work due to a disabling condition or impairment by providing a partial replacement wage (cash benefits). Although SSA bases the value of the replacement wage on a worker's past nominal earnings, the agency also indexes or adjusts the replacement wage to reflect changes in the average national wage level over time, as measured by the Average Wage Index (AWI). [76] As a result, a high relative replacement wage may encourage workers who have the ability to obtain some form of employment not to work and apply for SSDI instead.[77]

The influence of the relative replacement wage on an individual's decision to apply for SSDI may especially affect low-income workers, to the extent that said workers have experienced slower real income growth relative to medium and high-wage earners since 1980. Whereas the real earnings of low-income workers (10th percentile) grew 12% between 1980 and 2004, the real earnings of medium-income workers (50th percentile) and high-income workers (90th percentile) increased 15% and 36%, respectively.[78] The widening distribution of income during this period helped to expand the national AWI, thereby increasing the value of the indexed replacement wage for low-income workers relative to their slower growing real earnings.[79]

The combination of sluggish real wage growth and rising replacement rates may have impelled low-income workers to apply for SSDI as a means of enhancing their annual compensation. One study found that the "wage gap" between low-skilled workers with only a high school degree and workers with additional education accounted for 68.4% of the variation in SSDI applications between 1978 and 2008.[80] However, researchers are divided over the extent to which rising replacement wage rates induce low-income workers to apply for SSDI benefits.[81]

The Value of Health Care Benefits

Access to health care could also affect an individual's decision to apply for SSDI. Over the years, the cost of health insurance has grown considerably. Between 1999 and 2010, the average annual total premium (employer and employee) for family coverage rose 137.8% (from $5,791 to $13,770).[82] The marked increase in the cost of premiums has made it exceedingly difficult for many individuals and employers to continue paying for health insurance. From 1999 to 2010, the share of the population covered by private health insurance declined from 73.0% to 64.0%.[83] Because of the high cost of treating and managing chronic or severe medical conditions on their own, individuals with disabilities who lack health insurance may apply for SSDI in order to qualify for Medicare. Therefore, the rising cost of private medical insurance might have played a role in driving up the SSDI prevalence rate.[84]

However, the recently enacted Patient Protection and Affordable Care Act (ACA; P.L. 111-148, as amended) could help to reduce the number of individuals who apply for SSDI in order to qualify for Medicare in the future. ACA is designed to increase access to affordable health insurance for individuals without coverage and make health insurance more affordable for those already covered.[85] To expand the availability of affordable health insurance, ACA requires the establishment of state-based insurance exchanges for the purchase of health insurance and sets federal minimum requirements for the private health insurance market. Moreover, the act provides federal subsidies to certain individuals and families to reduce the cost of purchasing health insurance coverage, as well as expands eligibility for Medicaid. By making health insurance more affordable for individuals without coverage, ACA may reduce the incentives to apply for SSDI in order to qualify for Medicare, thereby abating the incidence of benefit receipt. Yet, it remains to be seen whether ACA will have a meaningful effect on the SSDI prevalence rate in the future.

A Lack of Consistency in the Initial Determination Process

As earlier noted, DDS examiners used a combination of medical, vocational, and functional evidence to determine whether a claimant's impairment precludes him or her from engaging in SGA.[86] Although DDS examiners base their initial determinations on uniform guidelines established by SSA, regional differences in demographic, health, and employment characteristics may produce variation in initial allowance rates between DDS offices.[87] However, a recent study by the RAND Corporation found an appreciable degree of variation in determination outcomes across examiners within the same DDS office.[88] The study estimated that up to 60% of applicants "could have received a different initial determination from at least one other examiner in the DDS office."[89] Even though the appeals process mitigated some of this variation, the study concluded that up to 23% of claimants could have ultimately received a different outcome had another examiner in the DDS office performed the determination.[90]

The uncertainty of an outcome at the initial determination level due to variation across DDS examiners may have encouraged denied claimants to pursue the appeals process, thereby increasing their likelihood of SSDI receipt. The aforementioned study found that claimants denied by strict examiners were more likely to appeal their determinations.[91] Between FY1986 and FY2010, the number of dispositions conducted by Administrative Law Judges (ALJ) at the hearing level increased 242.3% (from 215,489 to 737,616).[92] Although most of the awards granted by SSA during this period were made at the initial determination level, ALJs adjudicated the highest allowance rate of any level in the determination or appeals process.[93] In FY2010, the allowance rate at the hearing level was 62%, compared with 35% at the initial level, 13% at the reconsideration level, 2% at the Appeals Council level, and 4% at the federal court level.[94] The RAND study found that of the denied claimants who contested their initial determination, 75% had their denial overturned eventually on appeal.[95] The increased use of the appeals process due to variation across DDS examiners, coupled with higher allowance rates at the hearing level, may have contributed to the growth in the SSDI program.[96]

Changes in Federal Policy

The SSDI program of today looks quite different from the one created in 1956. At its inception, the program only provided cash benefits to workers aged 50 to 64 and disabled adult children whose disability began before the age of 18.[97] Since then, the program has expanded to cover dependents and workers under the age of 50, as well as provide health care for disabled-worker beneficiaries. The following subsection explores how legislative changes to both program eligibility criteria and OASI benefits in the early 1980s may have helped to enlarge SSDI rolls.

The Disability Benefits Reform Act of 1984

The Social Security Disability Amendments of 1980 (P.L. 96-265) vastly expanded the use of continuing disability reviews (CDR) as a means of reducing the growth in program costs. CDRs are periodic medical reevaluations to determine whether disabled beneficiaries continue to meet SSA's definition of disability. Between January 1982 and the fall of 1984, SSA issued benefit termination notices to 490,000 of the 1.2 million SSDI beneficiaries subjected to a CDR.[98] However, the rise in beneficiary terminations due to CDRs sparked a degree of public outcry and had "a very damaging effect on the public perception of SSA's administration of the disability program."[99] News stories at the time often depicted the economic and emotional difficulties faced by recently terminated beneficiaries and their dependents.[100] Ultimately, of the 490,000 beneficiaries who received termination notices because of CDRs, approximately 200,000 had their benefits reinstated on appeal.[101]

In response to the contention over the increased use of CDRs, Congress unanimously enacted a series of reforms to improve consistency and uniformity in the disability determination process.[102] The Disability Benefits Reform Act of 1984 (P.L. 98-460) changed the statutory standards for evaluating disability in a variety of ways. First, it revised the medical eligibility criteria for CDRs so that SSA can only terminate the benefits of a recipient due to a medical improvement if the agency finds substantial evidence demonstrating medical improvement related to the recipient's ability to work since his or her most recent favorable determination.[103] Under the 1980 amendments, SSA treated medical CDRs as a new determination and therefore did not evaluate a beneficiary's impairment relative to the previous determination. Second, it amended the mental disorders category of the *Listing of Impairments* to give greater weight to functional capabilities.[104] Before the reforms, disability determinations primarily relied on medical factors, which tended to disfavor claimants with mental impairments from benefit receipt. Third, it required SSA to consider the combined effect of multiple non-severe impairments on the claimant's ability to engage in SGA.[105] Prior to the 1984 amendments, a disability determination could not proceed unless the claimant had one or more independently severe impairments.[106]

In enacting the 1984 amendments, Congress effectively relaxed the eligibility criteria needed to qualify for SSDI—relative to the 1980 amendments—for certain diagnostic groups such as musculoskeletal and mental disorders. Whereas the revision of the *Listing of Impairments* to give greater weight to functional capabilities permitted more claimants with mental impairment to qualify for SSDI, the allowance of the combined effect of multiple non-severe impairments made it easier for claimants with musculoskeletal impairments to enroll in the program.[107] Consequently, the percent distribution of awards to disabled-worker beneficiaries by diagnostic group started to change over time.[108] As Figure 6 illustrates, the share of newly awarded beneficiaries with mental impairments increased from 10.3% in 1981 to 19.2% in 2011, whereas the portion of newly awarded beneficiaries with musculoskeletal impairments rose from 16.7% to 33.8% during the same period.[109]

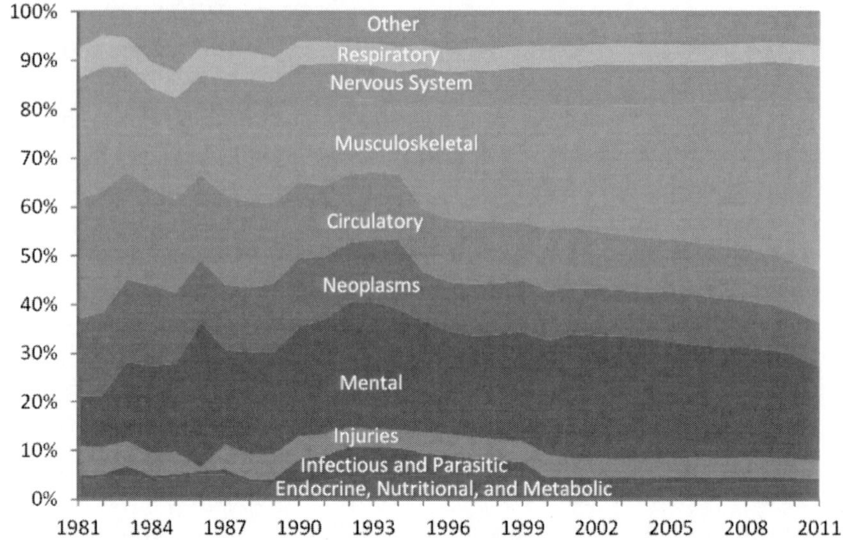

Source: Computed from the Social Security Administration, Annual Statistical Report on the Social Security Disability Insurance Program, 2011, Table 40, pp. 103-108.

Notes: For information on the diagnostic categories, please see the Listing of Impairments in the Social Security Administration publication Disability Evaluation Under Social Security, available at http://www.SSA.gov/disability/professionals/bluebook/. This publication is commonly referred to as the SSA Blue Book.

Figure 6. The Percent Distribution of Newly Awarded Disabled-Worker Beneficiaries; By Diagnostic Group (1981-2011).

The change in the percentage distribution of awards to disabled-worker beneficiaries by diagnostic group may have increased the program prevalence rate, insofar as beneficiaries with mental and musculoskeletal impairments stay on SSDI longer relative to beneficiaries with certain other impairments (e.g., injuries or infections).[110] Beneficiaries with mental or musculoskeletal impairments experience low mortality rates, moderate recovery rates, and high retirement conversation rates, all of which result in a long average duration of benefit receipt.[111] Moreover, since beneficiaries with mental impairments are typically younger, their time on SSDI rolls could last decades.[112]

The Social Security Amendments of 1983

Congress enacted the comprehensive Social Security Amendments of 1983 (P.L. 98-21) in response to the financial problems of the Old-Age and Survivors Insurance (OASI) trust fund identified by the National Commission on Social Security Reform.[113] To address the long-term sustainability of the OASI program, Congress incrementally increased the full retirement age (FRA) from 65 to 67, thereby expanding the maximum penalty for taking early retirement at age 62 from a 20% to a 30% reduction in cash benefits (based on year of birth).[114] The increase in FRA resulted in program savings that improved the solvency of the OASI trust fund.

However, the statutory changes to OASI eligibility rules may have also exacerbated the SSDI prevalence rate in three important ways. First, the increase in FRA expanded the share of potential SSDI applicants in their most disability-prone years (aged 50 and older). Between 2003 and 2012, the number of insured workers aged 65 to 66 rose from 228,000 to more than 2.4 million.[115] Since older workers suffer from higher disability rates, the increase in FRA likely pushed the SSDI incidence rate upward.[116] Second, the increase in FRA lengthened the duration of benefit receipt for recipients close to retirement age.[117] Prior to the 1983 amendments, SSA converted beneficiaries who turned age 65 from SSDI benefits to OASI retirement benefits. However, following the implementation of the amendments, beneficiaries aged 65 and older increasingly remained on SSDI longer, consequently aggravating the program prevalence rate. In December 2011, nearly 404,800 beneficiaries aged 65 to 66 received monthly SSDI payments from SSA.[118]

Third, the rise in the maximum penalty for early retirement increased the value of disability cash benefits. Since the maximum monthly full retired-worker benefit is the same as the maximum monthly disabled-worker benefit, the maximum value of an early retirement benefit at the age of 62 is 20%-30% less than the maximum value of a disability benefit, depending on year of birth. As a result, a growing number of OASDI insured workers aged 62 to FRA may have opted to apply for SSDI benefits in order to maximize their annual compensation. Recent studies suggest that the increasing value of disability benefits relative to early retirement benefits induces individuals to apply for SSDI benefits.[119] However, researchers are divided over the extent to which individuals aged 62 to FRA who apply for disability benefits based on their relative value to early retirement benefits actually receive an award from SSA.[120]

Overview of Reform Proposals

Since the effects of changes in the age-sex distribution of the population on SSDI rolls have for the most part run their course, SSA's Chief Actuary estimates that the cost and income to the DI trust fund as a percentage of GDP will stabilize over the long term.[121] However, the Chief Actuary projects the current gap between DI revenue and expenditures to remain persistent into the future.[122] Without appropriate action, the Office of the Chief Actuary estimates that the DI trust fund reserves will be depleted in 2016, at which point the trust fund will have only enough revenue to pay 79% of scheduled benefits.[123] To assist lawmakers in addressing the sustainability of the program, this section provides an overview of reform proposals to mitigate the prevalence of benefit receipt and thus reduce future program expenditures.[124] The selected proposals discussed in this section come from a variety of sources, including academic researchers, advocacy organizations, government agencies, and the Social Security Advisory Board.[125]

Stricter Eligibility Criteria

One policy option to reduce the growth in SSDI rolls is to tighten the eligibility requirements for program enrollment. In general, the aim of enhancing eligibility criteria is to mitigate the number of future awardees with some capacity to work (i.e., claimants on the margin of program entry), while continuing to grant awards to claimants with little or no ability to engage in substantial gainful activity (SGA). In theory, claimants on the edge of program entry could potentially work above SGA; therefore, stricter eligibility criteria may affect marginal claimants less adversely compared to more severely disabled claimants.[126] However, there is no guarantee that all the claimants on the margin of program entry have either the capacity or opportunity to engage in SGA. Thus, stricter eligibility criteria may inadvertently deny benefits to claimants with little or no ability to work at all. Although it is difficult to discern which type of claimants would be affected by more stringent eligibility requirements, a recent study found that marginal program entrants are more likely to be younger, suffer from mental impairments, and have low earnings histories.[127]

This subsection examines several options for increasing the eligibility criteria of the SSDI program, which the Congressional Budget Office (CBO) outlined and scored in its 2012 report, *Policy Options for the Social Security Disability Insurance Program.*[128]

Increase the Recency-of-Work Requirement

As mentioned earlier, to qualify for disability benefits, a worker must typically have 40 credits (quarters of coverage), 20 of which were earned in the last 10 years ending with the year of disability onset.[129] In other words, disability claimants must have generally worked five of the past 10 years to be eligible for SSDI. The recency-of-work requirement (sometimes known as the 20/40 rule) restricts the program to individuals who have worked of late and for a reasonable length of time in covered employment.[130]

CBO recently estimated the impact of increasing the recency-of-work requirement on beneficiary enrollment. The agency projected that requiring disability claimants to have worked four of the past six years (instead of five of the past 10) starting in 2013 would have reduced the number of SSDI beneficiaries by 4% in 2022, as well as decreased program outlays by $8.0 billion in that year.[131]

The stricter recency-of-work requirement would likely affect individuals with intermittent work histories, specifically workers with prolonged and sustained bouts of absence from covered employment due to unemployment or withdrawal from the labor force.[132] A recent study found that while men report leaving the labor force primarily because of disability, women typically report leaving the labor force to care for someone in their household.[133] Consequently, the more stringent recency-of-work requirement may disproportionately affect women who drop out of the labor force to act as caregivers.[134]

Adjust the Age Categories for Vocational Factors

As noted earlier, in addition to assessing an applicant's medical condition, DDS examiners also take into account the individual's ability to perform either any past relevant work or other work that exists in the national economy. Vocational factors such as age, education, and work experience—in combination with the individual's residual functional capacity—help an examiner to determine whether an applicant's impairment precludes him or her engaging in SGA. Since eligibility criteria based on education and work experience typically becomes less stringent with age, SSA is more likely to award benefits to older insured workers. Therefore, raising the upper age categories for vocational factors could mitigate the growth in the number of older beneficiaries (aged 45 to FRA) on SSDI rolls.

Currently, SSA categorizes older workers across four age ranges: 45-49, 50-54, 55-59, and 60 and older.[135] CBO examined the effects of increasing the 45-49 and 50-54 age ranges by two years to 47-51 and 52-56 and making 57 to

FRA the new maximum range, thereby eliminating the 45, 46, and 60 and older categories. According to CBO, implementing this policy option in 2013 would have decreased the number of SSDI beneficiaries by 50,000 or 0.5% in 2022, as well as reduced program expenditures by $1.0 billion in that year.[136]

Adjusting the age categories for vocational factors would likely encourage older insured workers to seek out other potential income supports. Whereas workers aged 62 to FRA could apply for early retirement benefits, workers with a recent attachment to the labor force may choose to apply for other work-related supports such as state workers' compensation, private disability insurance, or unemployment insurance. Meanwhile, low-income claimants would most likely apply for SSI and Medicaid in response to the adjustment in the age categories.[137]

SSA explored raising the age categories in the past but ultimately decided against it. In November 2005, SSA issued a Notice of Proposed Rulemaking (NPRM) that proposed to increase the age categories for older insured workers by two years.[138] However, after collecting feedback from the public, SSA withdrew the NPRM in May of 2009.[139]

Improved Program Administration

Another reform option is to augment program consistency and integrity to reduce the number of non-meritorious claimants on SSDI. Variation in the application of SSA guidelines can distort the disability determination and adjudication process, resulting in the agency granting awards to non-meritorious claimants or denying benefits to claimants with little or no capacity to work. Similarly, diminished program integrity—whether through waste, fraud, or abuse—may permit some beneficiaries to remain on SSDI in spite of their considerable work-related medical improvements. This subsection outlines reforms to the administration of the program that could conceivably reduce the growth in SSDI rolls.

Changing the Hearing Level Process from Inquisitorial to Adversarial

Claimants displeased with a determination at the reconsideration level of the appeals process may request a hearing before an Administrative Law Judge (ALJ), in writing, within 60 days upon receipt of the determination. At the hearing level, claimants may present additional evidence or arguments to support their case, as well as appoint a representative to act on their behalf (either an attorney or non-attorney). Since SSA is not represented at the hearing, the proceeding is considered inquisitorial or non-adversarial.[140] Under an inquisitorial process, ALJs investigate the merits of an appeal by informally questioning the claimant, as well as any scheduled witnesses (i.e., medical or vocational experts). Proponents of the inquisitorial process argue that the informal nature of the proceedings and lack of cross-examination by an opposing attorney creates an environment conducive to a claimant sharing the information needed by the ALJ to make an informed decision.[141]

However, opponents contend that inquisitorial process encumbers the ability of ALJs to make informed decisions on a consistent basis, inasmuch as the process forces ALJs to adjudicate appeals impartially while simultaneously representing the interests of both claimants and SSA.[142]

According to the Association of Administrative Law Judges (AALJ), having to wear all three "hats" during a hearing sometimes places an ALJ in an untenable situation, in which the judge must represent clients whose interests are at odds with one another.[143] Moreover, the difficulty of maintaining impartiality while simultaneously representing the interests of both parties may cause an ALJ to overlook a key piece of evidence or argument, consequently affecting the outcome of the decision.

To improve the accuracy of appeals at the hearing level, both AALJ and the Social Security Advisory Board (SSAB) advocate switching from an inquisitorial to an adversarial process in which claimants and SSA are each afforded representation.[144] The two organizations argue that the vigorous cross-examination of claimants by SSA representatives would provide ALJs with additional information and evidence with which to form their decisions, thereby creating greater consistency and accountability in the appeals process. According to SSAB, under the inquisitorial process, some ALJs may be reluctant to question claimants aggressively for fear of appearing to be biased.[145] This hesitation may prevent ALJs from discovering all the evidence necessary to make fully informed decisions, consequently affecting hearing outcomes. Therefore, adopting an adversarial model could allow ALJs to investigate the history and extent of claimants' medical impairments more thoroughly, resulting in better-reasoned decisions and greater judicial consistency.

The potential for improved consistency and accountability at the hearing level may help to lower the overall allowance rate and thus reduce the growth in SSDI rolls. A January 2013 audit report by SSA's Office of the Inspector General (OIG) discovered wide variances in the allowance rates among ALJs between and within hearing offices.[146] In addition, the report found a direct relationship between the number of cases adjudicated by ALJs (productivity) and allowance rates.[147] In other words, high-allowance ALJs adjudicated more dispositions relative to the office average, whereas low-allowance ALJs adjudicated fewer dispositions compared with the office average. By improving the quality of decisions, the adversarial process could theoretically help to attenuate large variances in the allowance rates among ALJs, subsequently mitigating the number of non-meritorious claimants awarded SSDI.

However, successfully implementing an adversarial process at the hearing level poses several challenges for SSA. First, switching from an inquisitorial to adversarial process would require additional expenditures to hire attorneys and appropriate staff. Disability hearings are already quite costly for SSA. In FY2011, the unit cost of adjudicating a disability hearing was $2,752.00, whereas the unit cost of processing an initial disability claim was only $1,058.44.[148] Even though SSA representation may eventually produce budgetary savings by reducing the allowance rate at the hearing level, the conversion to an adversarial process would still present SSA with substantial costs in the short term.

Second, it is unclear whether the adversarial process at the hearing level would survive a legal challenge from denied claimants, inasmuch a federal judge issued an injunction against SSA's previous adversarial pilot program in 1986.[149] Third, due to a paucity of research on the subject, the effects of switching to an adversarial process are highly ambiguous and difficult to discern. To assess the feasibility of switching to an adversarial process today, SSA may need to conduct another demonstration project to determine whether SSA representation at the hearing level could improve consistency and accountability in a cost-effective manner.[150]

Update SSA's Listing of Impairments

During the disability determination process, DDS examiners—with the help of medical and psychological consultants—typically use medical evidence collected from the claimant's physicians, hospitals, clinics, or other institutions of treatment to determine the severity of the claimant's impairment.[151] In order to assess whether the impairment precludes the claimant from working, DDS examiners evaluate the impairment against the *Listing of Impairments* (hereinafter "listings"), which categorizes SSA approved medical conditions for disability across 14 major body systems for adults.[152] SSA designed the listings to assist examiners in expediting claims by providing a uniform collection of medical conditions that prevent individuals from engaging in SGA. Most of the medical conditions contained in the listings are permanent or expected to result in death or a specific statement of duration.[153] If the claimant's impairment meets (or is of equal severity to) the criteria in the listings, SSA considers the claimant to have a work-limiting disability. Claimants who do not meet the medical criteria in the listings proceed to a more individualized assessment that examines their residual functional capacity to work, as well as vocational factors.[154]

Although the listings serve as a useful guide for DDS examiners, the percentage of awards determined by medical listings has decreased substantially over the years. According to SSAB, between FY1980 and FY2010, the share of initial allowances based on the claimant meeting the medical listings declined from 57.9% to 37.9%, whereas the portion of initial allowances based on the claimant having an impairment equal in severity fell from 16.2% to 7.9%.[155] Conversely, the percentage of initial allowances based on vocational considerations increased during this period from 25.9% to 54.3%.[156] SSAB, the Government Accountability Office (GAO), and SSA's OIG all attribute the decline in the percentage of cases decided based on the claimant's medical condition to the increasingly outdated nature of the medical listings. In 2000, OIG found that SSA had not updated certain listings in over 10 years; moreover, SSA had not updated the listings for mental disorders in 15 years.[157] In 2003, GAO identified SSDI as a high-risk program, inasmuch as the program relied on medical listings that did not reflect the impact of medical and technological advances on work-limiting medical conditions.[158]

SSAB has expressed concern over the shift in the basis for decision from medical listings to vocational factors, to the extent that cases decided based on vocational considerations may require a more substantial degree of subjectivity relative to cases determined based on medical listings.[159] In other words, determinations based primarily on carefully researched medical impairments may be less prone to individual examiner bias than cases decided using the claimant's residual functional capacity to work in the national economy. Indeed, the reduced reliance on medical listings may explain some of the aforementioned variation in initial disability determinations across DDS examiners.

To improve the quality and accuracy of disability determinations, SSA initiated a two-tiered process for updating its medical listings beginning in 2003.[160] Under the new process, the agency first completes a comprehensive revision of each listing category, taking into account any medical disorder or disease that may inhibit an individual's ability to work.[161] Once the comprehensive update is complete, SSA conducts periodic reviews of each listing category to ensure that the listings are current. According to SSA officials, the agency has completed comprehensive revisions to ten of the fourteen major adult body systems.[162] However, SSA has experienced delays in completing comprehensive updates to the remaining four major adult body systems.[163]

SSA has still not completed a final revision of the listing for mental disorders—SSDI's second most diagnosed impairment—despite the fact that the impairment category last received a comprehensive update in 1985.[164] SSA officials attribute the delay to a shortage of qualified staff, in addition to the enormous complexity of implementing and revising new medical listings.[165] The agency hopes to complete comprehensive revisions to the four remaining adult body systems by the end of FY2014.[166]

Updated medical listings that take into account medical and technological advances, as well as changes in the labor market, could allow DDS examiners to better identify individuals with severe work-limiting disabilities, while screening out non-meritorious claimants who could potentially engage in SGA. However, the impact of updated medical listings on the prevalence of benefit receipt remains unclear, in that claimants denied at the medical listings stage of the determination process may still be awarded SSDI at the subsequent vocational stages.

Update SSA's Occupational Information System

If a claimant fails to meet the eligibility criteria outlined in the medical listings, SSA will proceed with a more individualized assessment that examines the claimant's ability to engage in SGA. To "minimize subjectivity and promote national consistency," SSA employs a system of medical and vocational rules designed to assist examiners in discerning whether a claimant can perform either any past relevant work or other work that exists in the national economy.[167] SSA considers claimants who cannot perform any other work to be disabled and therefore eligible for SSDI.

Currently, SSA uses the Department of Labor's Dictionary of Occupation Titles (DOT) to determine the physical and mental demands of available work in the national economy; however, because DOT last received a major update in 1977, its occupational information is largely outdated and thus unrepresentative of the employment opportunities that exist in the modern U.S. economy.[168] Although the Department of Labor replaced DOT with a new database in 1998— known as the Occupational Information Network (O*NET)—SSA concluded that the new database's occupational information was insufficient to meet its requirements.[169] A recent Senate report expressed concern over SSA's use of DOT, in that the system's increasingly outdated occupational information may award benefits to claimants who could conceivably work in occupations not detailed in DOT.[170]

To improve program consistency, SSA established the Occupational Information Development Advisory Panel in December of 2008 to research and develop a new occupational information system (OIS) for use in the vocational stages of the disability determination process.[171] In July 2012, SSA signed an interagency agreement with the Bureau of Labor Statistics (BLS) to test the viability of using BLS' National Compensation Survey (NCS) to collect updated occupational data for the new OIS.[172] According to SSA, the agency plans to conduct ongoing testing and analysis of its data collection process in FY2013 and FY2014, with the expectation of implementing the new OIS starting in FY2016.[173]

In the future, SSA's updated OIS may help to mitigate the growth in SSDI rolls. According to SSA, the occupational information in DOT reflects an industrial economy, whereas today's economy has become more service oriented.[174] As a result, modern occupations that require less physical exertion may allow individuals with certain disabilities to remain in the labor force. By updating its OIS to reflect current jobs in the national economy, SSA could potentially reduce the incidence of benefit receipt.

However, not all individuals with disabilities have the capacity to work in today's highly competitive, albeit somewhat less physically demanding, job market.[175] For example, older individuals with disabilities may have difficulty adjusting to the intensity and pressure of many of today's employment opportunities, whereas individuals with less extensive education may be less suited to "cognitively demanding" work.[176] Thus, some individuals with disabilities may lack the capacity to perform any work in the national economy, even after taking into account updated occupational data.

Increase the Number of CDRs Performed by SSA

Unlike program consistency reforms that reduce the incidence of benefit receipt, program integrity policies such as continuing disability reviews (CDR) terminate the benefits of recipients who fail to adhere to program rules and requirements. Medical CDRs are periodic reevaluations to determine whether disabled beneficiaries continue to meet SSA's definition of disability. If SSA finds substantial evidence of medical improvement related to a beneficiary's ability to work, the agency may consider the beneficiary no longer disabled and subsequently terminate his or her benefits. Increasing the number of medical CDRs performed by SSA has the potential to expand the recovery rate of beneficiaries with work-related medical improvements and thus abate the growth in SSDI rolls.

Periodic medical evaluations are one of the most cost-effective tools for improving program integrity.[177] In FY2010, the 324,567 full medical CDRs performed by the agency resulted in 82,422 initial decisions to cease benefits, as well as 2,152 initial decisions to terminate benefits because of beneficiaries' failure to cooperate (FTC) with SSA during the disability review process. [178] After all appeals, SSA's Office of the Chief Actuary (OCAct) estimated that the CDRs conducted in FY2010 would ultimately terminate the benefits of 57,272 disabled-worker beneficiaries and their dependents.[179] For every $1.0 spent on CDRs in FY2010, OCAct estimated approximately $9.3 in future program savings.[180]

However, a significant reduction in funding for CDRs between FY2003 and FY2007 left SSA with fewer resources with which to conduct disability reviews, resulting in an accretive backlog of medical CDRs.[181] In March of 2010, SSA's OIG estimated a backlog of 1.5 million full medical CDRs at the end of FY2010.[182] Had SSA performed all full medical CDRs when they were originally scheduled between calendar years (CY) 2005 through CY2010, OIG estimated that the agency would have removed approximately 90,000 to 180,000 beneficiaries from the rolls, thereby avoiding between $1.3 billion to $2.6 billion in payments to SSI, SSDI, and concurrent beneficiaries.[183] In spite of recent efforts to address the backlog, SSA estimated 1.3 million pending CDRs at the end of FY2012.[184]

To address the mounting backlog of CDRs and enhance program integrity, advocacy organizations, academic researchers, and President Obama all have expressed their support for increasing CDR funding.[185] The Budget Control Act of 2011 (P.L. 112-25), which caps discretionary spending and increases the federal government's statutory debt limit, includes a provision to adjust the discretionary spending caps to permit additional appropriations to SSA for program integrity activities such as CDRs and SSI redeterminations.[186] In March 2013, SSA estimated that if Congress had appropriated the maximum amount allowed for program integrity activities in FY2012, the agency would have completed an additional 126,000 full medical CDRs, thereby saving approximately $800 million in SSDI, SSI, Medicare, and Medicaid expenditures between FY2012 and FY2022.[187] Alternatively, the President's FY2014 budget proposes replacing the discretionary spending caps established under the Budget Control Act of 2011 with a dedicated source of mandatory funding to enable SSA to conduct more CDRs and SSI redeterminations on a consistent basis.[188] According to the President's FY2014 budget, the requested

$1.227 billion in mandatory funding and $273 million in discretionary base funding would allow SSA to perform at least 650,000 CDRs and at least 2.6 million SSI redeterminations.[189]

Even with additional funding, increasing the number of CDRs poses a challenge for SSA. High attrition rates, hiring freezes, and employee furloughs have affected SSA's ability to process CDRs. In response to budget deficits, some states instituted furloughs or hiring freezes for state employees following the last recession, including DDS examiners.[190] The contraction in the number of DDS examiners limited SSA's ability to conduct determinations and contributed to the backlog of CDRs. To combat the reduction in state DDS examiners, SSA transferred a portion of disability cases from furloughed DDS offices to non-furloughed DDS offices in other states; in addition, the agency hired more than 2,600 DDS employees in FY2009 and FY2010.[191] However, due to an agency-wide hiring freeze starting in FY2011, SSA stopped DDS hiring in FY2011 and did only limited critical hiring in FY2012.[192] The reduction in DDS hiring between FY2011 and FY2012 coincided with high rates of attrition for existing DDS employees. In 2012, 15 field offices witnessed a 30% reduction in staff levels and nearly one-third of all field offices experienced attrition rates of more than 10%.[193] Because of the combination of attrition and hiring freezes, SSA lost more than 1,200 DDS employees in FY2011 and 1,025 DDS employees in FY2012.[194]

Although additional funding would augment SSA's ability to perform CDRs by allowing the agency to hire new examiners, the shortage of veteran examiners with the experience to conduct CDRs may prevent SSA from completing all scheduled disability reviews. Part of the problem stems from the fact that DDS examiners experience high rates of turnover. According to GAO, over 20% of DDS examiners hired between September of 1998 and January of 2006 left or were terminated within their first year.[195] Of the DDS examiners who remain, it takes on average two years of training and experience before SSA considers them to be fully trained.[196] Therefore, even if Congress appropriated additional funds immediately for SSA, it may take the agency years to reestablish a robust pool of highly experienced DDS examiners.

Return-to-Work Incentives

Another policy option to combat the growth in SSDI rolls is to provide stronger incentives for beneficiaries to return to the labor force. To encourage beneficiaries to return to the labor force, SSA allows beneficiaries to test their ability to work by participating in a 9-month Trial Work Period (TWP), during which participants may earn any amount within a rolling 60-month period without having their benefits terminated or reduced.[197] Moreover, SSA provides employment services to equip beneficiaries with the training and support structure needed to find employment in a competitive job market. In spite of the services offered by SSA, very few beneficiaries permanently leave the SSDI program. In 2011, SSA terminated the benefits of only 0.5% of all disabled-worker recipients due to earnings above SGA.[198] This subsection outlines policies that may help to increase the return-to-work rate of SSDI beneficiaries and thus reduce the average duration of benefit receipt.[199]

Increase Awareness of Return-to-Work Services

To address some of the barriers to employment faced by beneficiaries with disabilities, Congress enacted the Ticket to Work and Work Incentives Improvement Act of 1999 (P.L. 106-170), which established the Ticket to Work and Self-Sufficiency program (hereinafter "Ticket to Work").[200] Ticket to Work assists beneficiaries between the ages of 18 and 64 in returning to the labor force by providing a voucher or ticket for employment, vocational rehabilitation (VR), or other support services through public or private contractors known as Employment Networks (EN), as well as traditional State VR agencies (SVRA). Participation in the Ticket to Work program is voluntary, and ticket holders (beneficiaries) decide when and whether to assign a ticket to a particular EN or SVRA. Under the program, SVRAs and ENs receive payments from SSA for services provided to ticket holders based on specific work-related performances measures.

Thus far, the Ticket to Work program has met with little success. Although program participants are more likely to have employment relative to other beneficiaries, only about 2.2% of all "active" tickets issued by SSA are "in use" by beneficiaries (i.e., assigned to an EN or SVRA).[201] According to GAO, EN representatives partially attribute Ticket to Work's low beneficiary participation rate to "a lack of understanding and awareness of the program," while some disability-rights organizations contend that the fear of losing benefits may deter beneficiaries from taking part in the program.[202]

To improve the return-to-work rate of SSDI recipients, researchers Bonnie O'Day and David Stapleton have proposed testing early intervention policies that provide beneficiaries with employment and other support services shortly after receipt of benefits.[203] The researchers argue that current employment services such as Ticket to Work have failed to increase the return-towork rate, inasmuch as many beneficiaries "have been separated from the labor force, often for years, before they are offered assistance."[204] By providing beneficiaries with employment and other support services earlier during their stay on SSDI (i.e., when their attachment to the labor force is relatively strong), the researchers posit that said beneficiaries may have a greater chance of returning to work.

One early intervention option is to require all future beneficiaries to participate in mandatory work preparation counseling in order to educate them on the variety of return-to-work services offered by SSA.[205] Mandatory counseling has the potential to elucidate beneficiary confusion regarding return-to-work services, which may in turn increase the likelihood of beneficiary participation in programs such as Ticket to Work. Although mandatory work preparation counseling would require new funding to hire additional SSA affiliated counselors, the counseling may be cost-effective if it improves the return-to-work rate of SSDI recipients.

To demonstrate the benefits of early intervention, O'Day and Stapleton point to the United Kingdom's (UK's) recently discontinued Pathways to Work program as an example of how mandatory participation in work preparation can improve beneficiary employment outcomes.[206] Like Ticket to Work, Pathways to Work was designed to encourage beneficiaries with disabilities to return to work by providing employment support services. Although participation in Pathways to Work was voluntary, starting in 2008, new beneficiaries were required to participate in six Work Focused Interviews (WFI), during which advisors provided beneficiaries with information on optional employment services and financial incentives for returning to work.[207] A cost-benefit analysis conducted by the UK's Department of Work and Pensions concluded that WFIs and return-to-work tax credits were the most expensive components of Pathways to Work; however, the study noted that the program ultimately yielded a net societal benefit of £3.06 ($5.56) for every £1.00 ($1.82) invested in Pathways to Work.[208] Another study found that the Pathways to Work program increased the probability of a beneficiary having a job by 7.4 percentage points.[209]

Currently, SSA oversees two voluntary grant programs aimed at increasing beneficiary awareness of return-to-work services. In addition to the Ticket to Work program, P.L. 106-170 also established the Work Incentives Planning and Assistance (WIPA) program and the Protection and Advocacy for Beneficiaries of Social Security (PABSS).[210] The WIPA program awards grants to community organizations that provide education and assistance for beneficiaries interested in returning to work, whereas the PABSS program provides grants for legal assistance and advice on how to obtain VR, employment, or other services for work-oriented beneficiaries.

Estimating the overall impact of mandatory counseling on the SSDI beneficiary return-to-work rate is difficult because the results of SSA's current employment-counseling initiatives are inconclusive. According to one study, the use of WIPA services possibly has a positive effect on the employment outcomes of SSI/SSDI beneficiaries; however, the study's researchers cautioned against drawing a causal relationship between receipt of WIPA services and employment outcomes.[211] In essence, the researchers were unable to discern whether beneficiaries who received WIPA services would have enjoyed the same employment outcome in the absence of such assistance.

In addition, program rules concerning eligibility and benefit levels could make SSDI less responsive to the positive effects of mandatory counseling relative to other disability programs, such as the United Kingdoms's.[212] According to O'Day and Stapleton, SSDI benefits are significantly more generous compared with UK incapacity benefits; moreover, SSDI's stricter eligibility requirements suggest that SSDI beneficiaries are less likely to have some residual functional capacity to work relative to UK beneficiaries.[213] Therefore, SSDI beneficiaries presumably have less incentive to return to work. Although mandatory counseling could improve the return-to-work rate of SSDI beneficiaries, the effect may be smaller compared with the impact of WFIs on UK beneficiary employment outcomes.

Benefit Offset

Another reason behind the low return-to-work rate stems from the fact that some beneficiaries deliberately "park" their earnings from work below the SGA threshold. After completing the TWP and 36-month Extended Period of Eligibility (EPE), beneficiaries must earn below SGA or risk having their benefits terminated.[214] Consequently, some beneficiaries may intentionally keep their earnings below SGA in order to maintain receipt of SSDI benefits. One study found that between 0.2% and 0.4% of all SSDI beneficiaries parked their earnings below SGA in a typical month from 2002 to 2006.[215]

Beneficiaries may park their earnings below SGA (sometimes called the "cash cliff"), in part, because their impairment prevents them from returning to work on a consistent basis. Another study found that 59.0% of Ticket to Work participants returned to work at some point between 2003 and 2005; however, of those participants who left work, the most cited reason was due to poor health.[216] Parking earnings below SGA may weaken a work-oriented beneficiary's attachment to the labor force, possibly resulting in an erosion of skills and thus a reduced likelihood of returning to work following a health-related withdrawal from the labor force.[217]

To remedy the phenomenon of parked earnings, some disability-rights organizations have advocated eliminating the fixed cash cliff (SGA threshold) and instead adopting a gradual benefit-offset model that allows beneficiaries to increase their earnings while remaining on SSDI.[218] The SSI program operates under a benefit-offset system, deducting $1 in benefits for every $2 in earned income above $65.[219] Benefit offset has the potential to reduce the average duration of benefit receipt, by increasing the time spent off SSDI rolls for beneficiaries engaged in work. Hence, benefit offset could lower overall SSDI program costs, while increasing beneficiary earnings and attachment to the labor force.

Benefit Offset National Demonstration

SSA is currently in the process of conducting a Benefit Offset National Demonstration (BOND) project, during which treatment participants lose $1 in benefits for every $2 in earnings exceeding a BOND Yearly Amount (BYA) equal to 12 times the monthly SGA amount.[220] BOND participants can also receive Enhanced Work Incentives Counseling (EWIC), which is designed address a range of issues related to returning to work, including access to medical treatment, employment services, and job training.[221] In implementing BOND, SSA seeks to test whether benefit offset can increase earnings and reduce dependence on SSDI for work-oriented beneficiaries (i.e., beneficiaries with some, albeit limited, capacity to work).[222]

In preparation for BOND, SSA implemented a four-state pilot program known as the Benefit Offset Pilot Demonstration (BOPD) from 2005 until the end of 2008.[223] According to SSA, participation in BOPD had a positive effect on the earnings of individuals in the treatment group; however, BOPD also increased mean benefit payments due to partial payments made to beneficiaries whose benefits would have been suspended under normal program rules for earning above SGA.[224]

In addition to increasing beneficiary earnings, BOND could conceivably increase the return-towork rate and therefore abate the growth in SSDI rolls. For example, beneficiaries with an above average likelihood of recovery but whose impairment results in considerable employment instability would benefit from the BOND program through increased labor force attachment. Under BOND program rules, said beneficiaries could maximize their potential labor force participation while they recover from their impairment, thereby increasing their likelihood of one day permanently returning to work.

Promote Supported-Work Policies

Some researchers have suggested shifting the focus of SSDI reform away from reducing the current beneficiary population toward policies designed to attenuate the inflow of beneficiaries into the program.[225] Advocates of this approach, sometimes referred to as "supported work," argue that offering employment supports shortly after the onset of disability would allow more workers who experience disability to remain attached to the labor force and therefore less likely to apply for SSDI. Most supported-work policies use financial incentives to encourage employers to provide preventative, accommodative, rehabilitative, and other return-to-work services as a means of reducing employee enrollment in the SSDI program. Although Title I of the Americans with Disabilities Act (ADA; P.L. 101-336, as amended) requires employers to provide some level of "reasonable accommodation" for employees with disabilities in the workplace, some employers fail to comply with the provisions of ADA, creating a barrier to employment for many workers with disabilities.[226] Faced with few employment opportunities, individuals with disabilities who could conceivably work given appropriate accommodation may turn to SSDI as a last resort. This subsection provides an overview of two supported-work policies that have the potential to slow the incidence of benefit receipt and thus reduce the growth in disability rolls.

Experience Rate the Employer's Portion of the Payroll Tax

Experience rating is a process for determining insurance premiums based on the cost of an insurance pool's past claims. In essence, an insurer calculates a firm's insurance premium based on the likelihood, or risk, of the firm submitting a future claim given its previous behavior. Many types of employer-sponsored insurance use experience rating to determine premiums, including state workers' compensation (WC), unemployment insurance (UI), and private disability insurance (PDI).[227] By making premiums a function of past claims, experience rating adjusts the firm's costs to reflect its use of the insurance program. Consequently, experience rating creates financial incentives for employers to prevent employees from needing specific insurance services in the first place.

To reduce the incidence of SSDI receipt, researchers Richard V. Burkhauser, Mary C. Daly, and Philip R. de Jong have suggested that the federal government should implement some form of experience rating to the employer's portion of the payroll tax used to fund SSDI and Medicare.[228] Currently, employers pay the same payroll tax rate on their employees' earnings for SSDI, regardless of the rate at which their employees enroll in the program.[229] Under the current system, employers have little incentive to make robust investments in preventative, accommodative, or rehabilitative services, because employees with disabilities can transition to SSDI without any additional cost to the employer. However, under an experience rated system, employers whose employees enroll in SSDI at rates above the national average would pay a higher payroll tax rate, whereas firms whose employees enter the program at below average rates would pay a lower payroll tax rate. In theory, the experienced-rated payroll tax should incentivize employers to provide supported-work services, in order to reduce their employees' enrollment rate in SSDI and subsequently lower their labor costs.

Supporters of experience rating often point to its implementation in the Netherland's disability insurance (DI) system as evidence of its potential impact in the United States. Between 1998 and 2003, the Netherlands gradually incorporated experience rating into its DI system, charging Dutch employers a differentiated premium rate based on their employees' past enrollment in the DI system.[230] According to one empirical study, the effect of instituting experience-rated DI premiums amounted to a 15% reduction in the enrollment of workers in the Dutch DI program.[231] Since the early 2000s, the Netherlands has witnessed a marked decline in its DI prevalence rate.[232]

Another potential advantage of the experience rating option is its relative simplicity. Employers already report payroll tax data to the Internal Revenue Service (IRS), which the agency shares with SSA. Moreover, most employers are accustomed to the concept of experience rating stemming from their experience paying state WC and UI premiums. By compiling both payroll tax and beneficiary award data, SSA could conceivably initiate an experience rating system to the SSDI payroll tax "without imposing substantial new reporting requirements or administrative burdens on employers."[233]

Notwithstanding the potential for reduced enrollment in SSDI, implementing an experience rating system to the employer's portion of the payroll tax may adversely affect some workers. For example, experience-rated payroll taxes could make employers hesitant to hire or retain workers "perceived to be a high risk for disability."[234] Employers may discriminate against older workers, people with chronic conditions such as diabetes, or individuals prone to at-risk behaviors (e.g., alcohol or substance abuse) in order to avoid paying a higher payroll tax rate on their employees' earnings. To address this possibility, supporters of experience rating suggest implementing risk adjustments specific to factors such as age, occupation, and health status, as well as enforcing existing anti-discrimination laws.[235]

In addition, experience rating could conceivably reduce the compensation or employment opportunities of low-wage workers. Some employers subject to higher payroll tax rates could shift the additional cost onto workers in the form of reduced take-home pay and benefits. Alternatively, employers unable to shift additional labor costs onto their employees may instead offset the higher payroll tax rate by hiring fewer workers in the future.[236] Since many low-wage individuals typically tend to work in professions with high rates of disability, they may be disproportionately affected by employer cost avoidance and therefore more likely to suffer financially as a result.[237] Opponents of experience rating argue that workers adversely affected by employer cost avoidance could turn to SSDI as a last resort, thereby increasing worker enrollment in the SSDI program.[238]

Furthermore, some critics of experience rating have expressed concern that while the system changes the incentives of employers with respect to program enrollment, it fails to address the incentives of workers to apply for SSDI.[239] Some workers may apply for SSDI because of economic circumstances such as unemployment or low wages.[240] Although the initial determination process screens out most non-meritorious claimants, SSA may grant awards to some claimants on the margin of program entry who could potentially work but choose not to due to economic circumstances. Under an experience rating system, the former employers of these new beneficiaries could have their payroll tax rate increased, even though the beneficiaries based their decision to apply for SSDI primarily on factors unrelated to health status or disability. As a result, said employers would be penalized twice for terminating a worker, insofar as their UI rate would increase, as well as their payroll tax rate for SSDI and Medicare. Given this scenario, opponents contend that experience rating the employer's portion of the payroll tax does little to address the moral hazard of workers applying to the program for reasons unrelated to health status or disability.[241]

Employer-Sponsored Private Disability Insurance

Another policy option to stem the flow of beneficiaries into SSDI is for the federal government to promote employer-sponsored private disability insurance (PDI). PDI provides beneficiaries with a partial wage replacement, as well as workplace accommodation, rehabilitation, and other returnto-work services. As of March 2012, 39% of all workers in private industry had access to short-term disability insurance, whereas 33% of said workers had access to long-term PDI.[242] Short-term PDI typically lasts a fixed number of weeks or months, whereas long-term disability insurance can last anywhere from a year to FRA.[243] Compared with other forms of employer-sponsored insurance such as health-care, PDI is relatively inexpensive.[244] In addition, employers can partially offset the cost of PDI by requiring employees to contribute to the plan.[245]

Some researchers have advocated that the federal government should promote employer-sponsored PDI to reduce the growth in SSDI rolls.[246] Employer-sponsored PDI plans have the potential to reduce the incidence of SSDI benefit receipt, inasmuch as they provide employment-support services soon after the onset of disability when the likelihood of recovery is highest. By intervening with robust supported-work services early in the disability process, PDI may keep workers with disabilities attached to the labor force and therefore less likely to apply for SSDI.[247]

The promotion of employer-sponsored PDI could come about in either one of two ways: (1) encouragement through incentives or (2) a government mandate. Under the former option, the federal government would offer employers financial incentives to provide PDI for their employees. For example, if the federal government adopted an experience rating system to the employer's portion of the SSDI and Medicare payroll tax, SSA could further lower the payroll tax rate of employers who purchase PDI and whose insurance agents coordinate with SSA officials (gatekeepers) to manage disability cases in a cost-effective manner.[248] Alternatively, the federal government could award subsidies or tax credits to firms that provide PDI.[249]

Under the latter option, the federal government would require all employers to provide PDI for their employees. To enforce the mandate, employers who fail to provide PDI would likely face financial penalties for their non-compliance. In 2010, only New Jersey, New York, Hawaii, and Puerto Rico required employers to provide some form of short-term PDI—known as temporary disability insurance (TDI)—or contribute to a state-operated fund.[250] Employer-mandated PDI, however, has become an increasingly popular approach to finance disability insurance in many European countries. The Netherlands, for example, now requires employers to cover the cost of sick pay for the first two years following the onset of a disabling condition, whereas the U.K. requires employers to pay up to six-months of statutory sick pay.[251]

Researchers David H. Autor and Mark Duggan have proposed requiring all employers to provide medium-term PDI, through which workers with disabilities would receive rehabilitation services, workplace accommodation, and a partial wage replacement for two years.[252] Plans under this proposal would be purchased on the existing PDI market, and employers would be permitted to require employees to contribute up to 40% of the cost of their coverage.[253] Following the exhaustion of employer-sponsored PDI, SSA would transition beneficiaries who still lack the ability to engage in SGA onto SSDI. Workers with extremely severe or terminal disabilities would be exempt from the two-year PDI requirement and would instead be immediately fast-tracked onto SSDI.[254]

Each approach to promoting PDI has its strengths and weaknesses. The financial incentives approach is advantageous, to the extent that its implementation would be simple by comparison. The federal government already encourages employers to hire workers with disabilities by offering tax credits to offset any workplace accommodation that workers with disabilities may require.[255] Therefore, expanding employer incentives to provide PDI via tax credits would entail minimal additional resources to institute. Although establishing SSA gatekeepers to work with employers and insurers under an experience rating system would likely require significantly more resources relative to the tax credit proposal, the net cost to the government could be limited, depending on the structure of the experience rating system.

In spite of these advantages, the voluntary nature of the financial incentives approach may not induce enough employers to purchase PDI plans to have an appreciable impact on the incidence of SSDI receipt. As noted above, the federal government currently offers employers tax incentives to hire workers with disabilities; however, the evidence that such incentives actually drive employers to hire said workers has been "limited and inconclusive."[256] Similarly, the lure of a lower payroll tax rate under an experience-rating model may not cause employers to purchase PDI, especially if the cost of providing PDI outweighs the savings from the reduced payroll tax rate.

On the other hand, the government mandate approach solves many of the inducement-related problems associated with voluntary financial incentives. After all, the prospect of having to pay financial penalties due to non-compliance is a more powerful incentive for employers relative to optional tax credits.[257] A government mandate under this approach, however, does not necessarily guarantee universal compliance because employers could opt out of carrying PDI by simply paying the appropriate penalty. Nevertheless, the increased incentive for employers to provide PDI may have an appreciable effect on the inflow of beneficiaries into the SSDI program.

However, it is difficult to discern whether a government mandate to require employers to provide PDI is economically feasible using the existing PDI market. Currently, most private disability insurers sell PDI plans as either short term (around 26 weeks) or long term (anywhere from a year to FRA).

Although both types of PDI cost employers about the same amount per-hour worked, long-term disability (LTD) insurance plans typically have stricter eligibility standards. For instances, LTD plans may have more stringent definitions of disability or more expansive exclusionary criteria concerning pre-existing medical conditions compared with short-term disability (STD) insurance.

Private disability insurers often incorporate stricter eligibility standards into their LTD plans because such plans are inherently riskier. After all, a LTD beneficiary could potentially receive benefits for years or even decades. To offset some of the risk associated with LTD plans, insurers often require beneficiaries to apply for SSDI after the onset of disability. Insurers deduct any subsequent SSDI income from a beneficiary's LTD benefit, thereby reducing their exposure to loss.

Therefore, mandated medium-term PDI plans—as outlined in the Autor and Duggan proposal— may not be financially viable in the current PDI market, to the extent that such plans do not permit insurers to offset part of their costs by requiring beneficiaries to apply for SSDI. While the increase in revenue stemming from more insurable workers may partially negate some of the increased risk of insuring people for disability over a longer period, it remains to be seen whether the PDI market can produce an economically feasible medium-term PDI plan.

APPENDIX. ACRONYMS

AALJ	Association of Administrative Law Judges
ADA	Americans with Disabilities Act
ACA	Patient Protection and Affordable Care Act
AIP	Adjudicatory Improvement Project
ALJ	Administrative Law Judge
APE	Aarts de Jong Wilms Goudriaan Public Economics
AWI	Average Wage Index
BEA	Bureau of Economic Analysis
BLS	Bureau of Labor Statistics
BOND	Benefit Offset National Demonstration
BOPD	Benefit Offset Pilot Demonstration
BPAO	Benefits Planning Assistance and Outreach Program
BYA	BOND Yearly Amount
CBO	Congressional Budget Office

CDR	Continuing Disability Review
COLA	Cost-of-Living Adjustment
CPI-W	Consumer Price Index for Urban Wage Earners and Clerical Workers
CPI- U	Consumer Price Index for All Urban Consumers
CPS	Current Population Survey
CY	Calendar Year
DA&A	Drug Addiction and Alcoholism
DDS	Disability Determination Service
DI	Disability Insurance
DOT	Dictionary of Occupational Titles
EITC	Earned Income Tax Credit
EN	Employment Network
EPE	Extended Period of Eligibility
EWIC	Enhanced Work Incentives Counseling
FICA	Federal Insurance Contributions Act
FRA	Full Retirement Age
FTC	Failure to Cooperate
FY	Fiscal Year
GAO	Government Accountability Office
GDP	Gross Domestic Product
HI	Hospital Insurance
IRS	Internal Revenue Service
LTD	Long-Term Disability
NBER	The National Bureau of Economic Research
NCS	National Compensation Survey
NPRM	Notice of Proposed Rulemaking
O*NET	Occupational Information Network
OASDI	Old-Age, Survivors and Disability Insurance
OASI	Old-Age and Survivors Insurance
OCAct	Office of the Chief Actuary
OIG	Office of the Inspector General
OIS	Occupational Information System
PABSS	Protection and Advocacy for Beneficiaries of Social Security
PDI	Private Disability Insurance
SECA	Self-Employment Contributions Act
SGA	Substantial Gainful Activity
SMI	Supplementary Medical Insurance
SSA	Social Security Administration

SSAB	Social Security Advisory Board
SSARP	Social Security Administration's Representation Project
SSDI	Social Security Disability Insurance
SSI	Supplemental Security Income
STD	Short-Term Disability
SVRA	State Vocational Rehabilitation Agency
TDI	Temporary Disability Insurance
TWP	Trial Work Period
UI	Unemployment Insurance
U.K.	United Kingdom
VR	Vocational Rehabilitation
WC	Workers' Compensation
WFI	Work-Focused Interviews
WIPA	Work Incentives Planning and Assistance

End Notes

[1] See, for example: U.S. Congress, House Committee on Ways and Means, Subcommittee on Social Security, *First in a Hearing Series on Securing the Future of the Social Security Disability Insurance Program*, 112th Cong., 1st sess., December 2, 2011, Serial 112–SS11, pp. 4-5, http://www.gpo.gov/fdsys/pkg/CHRG-112hhrg76319/pdf/CHRG112hhrg76319.pdf.

[2] For beneficiary data, see Social Security Administration, *Benefits Awarded by Type of Beneficiary*, http://www.ssa.gov/OACT/ProgData/icp.html. For insured worker data, see Social Security Administration, *Disability Insured Workers*, http://www.ssa.gov/oact/STATS/table4c2DI.html.

[3] Social Security Administration, *DI Trust Fund, A Social Security Fund*, http://www.ssa.gov/oact/STATS/ table4a2.html. Inflation-adjusted figures computed using the seasonally-unadjusted Consumer Price Index for All Urban Consumers (CPI-U) from the Bureau of Labor Statistics at ftp://ftp.bls.gov/pub/special.requests/cpi/cpiai.txt. Figures are in 2011 dollars.

[4] U.S. Congress, House Committee on Ways and Means, *The 2012 Annual Report of the Board of Trustees of the Federal Old-Age, Survivors Insurance and Federal Disability Insurance Trust Funds*, prepared by the Board of Trustees, Federal Old-Age and Survivors Insurance and Federal Disability Insurance Trust Funds, 112th Cong., 2nd sess., April 25, 2012, H.Doc. 112-102 (Washington: GPO, 2012), pp. 2-4, http://www.ssa.gov/oact/TR/2012/index.html, (hereinafter cited as "2012 Board of Trustees Report"). For more information on trust fund exhaustion, see CRS Report RL33514, *Social Security: What Would Happen If the Trust Funds Ran Out?*, by Christine Scott.

[5] For information on the Old-Age and Survivors Insurance (OASI) and DI trust funds, see CRS Report RL33028, *Social Security: The Trust Fund*, by Dawn Nuschler and Gary Sidor.

[6] For more information on the SSDI program, see CRS Report RL32279, *Primer on Disability Benefits: Social Security Disability Insurance (SSDI) and Supplemental Security Income (SSI)*, by Umar Moulta-Ali.

[7] 20 C.F.R. § 404.130(b). For more information on work history requirements, see Social Security Administration, *How You Earn Credits*, http://www.ssa.gov/pubs/10072.html. In 2013, a worker can receive one credit for each $1,160 of earnings, up to the maximum of four credits per year.

[8] See 20 C.F.R. § 404.130(c) and (d). Typically, individuals aged 24 to 30 who become disabled need quarters of coverage (work credits) in at least one-half of the quarters during the period ending with that quarter and beginning with the quarter after the quarter they became 21 years old. Individuals under the age of 24 generally must have at least 6 quarters of coverage in the 12-quarter period ending with the quarter in which their disability began.

[9] 42 U.S.C. § 423(d)(1)(A).

[10] See Social Security Administration, *Substantial Gainful Activity*, http://www.ssa.gov/oact /cola/sga.html.

[11] 20 C.F.R. § 404.211(e)(3).

[12] 20 C.F.R. § 404.272(a)(1). The COLA is measured as the percentage increase in the CPI-W from the third quarter of the year in which the last COLA increase became effective to the third quarter of the current year (see 20 C.F.R. § 404.274[b][ii]). For 2013, a 1.7% COLA was applied to benefits. For more information on COLA increases, see CRS Report 94-803, *Social Security: Cost-of-Living Adjustments*, by Gary Sidor.

[13] 20 C.F.R. § 404.408(a)(1)(i). In addition, cash benefits to dependents may be subject to certain maximum family benefit limits (see 20 C.F.R. § 404.403).

[14] The first month counted as part of the waiting period can be no more than 17 months before the month of application. For additional information on the five-month waiting period, see CRS Report RS22220, *Social Security Disability Insurance (SSDI): The Five-Month Waiting Period for Benefits*, by Umar Moulta-Ali.

[15] Social Security Administration, *Benefits Awarded by Type of Beneficiary*, http://www.ssa.gov /OACT/ProgData/ icp.html.

[16] For more information on Medicare coverage for SSDI beneficiaries, see CRS Report RS22195, *Social Security Disability Insurance (SSDI) and Medicare: The 24-Month Waiting Period for SSDI Beneficiaries Under Age 65*, by Scott Szymendera.

[17] For more information on SSI requirements, see CRS Report RL32279, *Primer on Disability Benefits: Social Security Disability Insurance (SSDI) and Supplemental Security Income (SSI)*, by Umar Moulta-Ali.

[18] SSA offsets SSI benefits based on receipt of other public benefits, including SSDI cash benefits. For more information, see CRS Report RS20294, *Supplemental Security Income (SSI): Income/Resource Limits and Accounts Exempt from Benefit Determinations*, by Umar Moulta-Ali.

[19] Social Security Administration, *Annual Statistical Report on the Social Security Disability Insurance Program, 2011*, 2012, Table 65, p. 157, http://www.ssa.gov/policy/docs /statcomps/di_asr/2011/index.html (hereinafter cited as "SSDI Annual Report 2011").

[20] Claimants may also apply for SSDI by telephone or mail. For more information on the SSDI determination and adjudication process, see CRS Report R41289, *Disability Benefits Available Under the Social Security Disability Insurance (SSDI) and Veterans Disability Compensation (VDC) Programs*, by Umar Moulta-Ali.

[21] 42 U.S.C. § 405.

[22] 20 C.F.R. § 404.1700. Claimants may be represented by either an attorney or non-attorney during the appeals process (as defined in 20 C.F.R. § 404.1705).

[23] See SSDI Annual Report 2011, p. 4. In 1999, SSA eliminated the reconsideration step in 10 States, as part of the Disability Redesign Prototype (Prototype) initiative, which included Alaska, Alabama, California (Los Angeles West and North Branches), Colorado, Louisiana, Michigan, Missouri, New Hampshire, New York, and Pennsylvania. Although SSA expected the initiative to result in earlier decisions and shorter wait-times for claimants, the opposite has been true. In fiscal year (FY) 2011, SSA reinstated the reconsideration step in the state of Michigan and is evaluating potential reinstatements in Colorado and other states. For more information, see CRS Report R41289, *Disability Benefits Available Under the Social Security Disability Insurance (SSDI) and Veterans Disability Compensation (VDC) Programs*, by Umar Moulta-Ali.

[24] Social Security Administration, *Annual Statistical Supplement to the Social Security Bulletin, 2012*, February 2013, Table 6.C7, http://www.ssa.gov/policy/docs/statcomps/supplement/2012/6c.html (hereinafter cited as "SSA Annual Statistical Supplement 2012").

[25] SSA typically measures the award rate by dividing awards by all applications minus pending claims. For more information on the award rate, see SSDI Annual Report 2011, Table 59, pp. 142-143.

[26] The Social Security Board of Trustees measures the disability enrollment (incidence) rate as "the ratio of the number of new beneficiaries awarded benefits each year to the number of individuals who meet insured requirements but are not yet receiving benefits (the disability-exposed population)." For more information on the incidence rate, see 2012 Board of Trustees Report, p. 125.

[27] Recipients whose cash benefits were terminated due to earnings above SGA may still be eligible for up to 93 months of premium-free Medicare Part A (Hospital Insurance) following a Trial Work Period (TWP). See SSDI Annual Report 2011, p. 6. For more information on return-to-work incentives and TWP, see the subsection of the report entitled "Return-to-Work Incentives."

[28] Tim Zayatz, *Social Security Disability Insurance Program Workers Experience: Actuarial Study No. 114*, Social Security Administration, 1999, Table 5, and subsequent editions, http://www.ssa.gov/oact/NOTES/actstud.html.

[29] Donna L. Hoyert, *75 Years of Mortality in the United States, 1935–2010*, Centers for Disease Control and Prevention: National Center for Health Statistics, 2012, http://www.cdc.gov/nchs/data/databriefs/db88.htm.

[30] FRA is currently 66; however, FRA will reach 67 for workers born in 1960 or later. For more information on FRA, see CRS Report R42035, *Social Security Primer*, by Dawn Nuschler.

[31] For more information on the Social Security Disability Amendments of 1980, see John R. Kearney, "Social Security and the "D" in OASDI: The History of a Federal Program Insuring Earners Against Disability," *Social Security Bulletin*, vol. 66 no. 3 (August 2006), http://www.ssa.gov/policy/docs/ssb/v66n3/v66n3p1.html (hereinafter cited as "Kearney 2006").

[32] Non-permanently disabled beneficiaries with a reasonable chance of recovery receive a CDR every three years. Disabled beneficiaries with a high probability of medical improvement typically receive a CDR at intervals between 6 months and 18 months following their most recent decision. Disabled beneficiaries with a low probability of medical improvement (permanently disabled) receive CDRs less frequently, generally at intervals determined by the Social Security Commissioner (normally every five to seven years). For more information, see 20 C.F.R. § 404.1590.

[33] According to SSA officials, the rise in the termination rate during the early 1980s is not entirely attributable to the accelerated use of CDRs. An initiative begun in 1981 by SSA aggressively targeted beneficiaries whom the agency believed were unlikely to have a disability or impairment, despite being on the rolls. This initiative, coupled with the increased use of CDRs, resulted in an increase in the recovery rate for SSDI beneficiaries in the early 1980s. For more information, see U.S. Government Accountability Office, *Social Security Disability Programs: Clearer Guidance Could Help SSA Apply the Medical Improvement Standard More Consistently*, GAO-07-8, October 3, 2006, p. 6, "The Disability Benefits Reform Act of 1984", http://www.gao.gov/products/GAO-07-8.

[34] Kearney 2006, p. 16.

[35] The Disability Benefits Reform Act of 1984 enshrined some of the 1983 reforms into law. For more information on how the 1984 amendments affected program participation, see the subsection of the report entitled "The Disability Benefits Reform Act of 1984."

[36] The act stopped awarding benefits to DA&A claimants on the day of enactment, March 29, 1996. DA&A beneficiaries who appealed the termination continued to receive benefits while they waited for a decision. For more information, see Paul Davies, Howard Iams, and Kalman Rupp, "The Effect of Welfare Reform on The SSA's Disability Programs: Design of Policy Evaluation and Early Evidence," *Social Security Bulletin*, vol. 63 no. 1 (July 2000), p. 4, http://www.ssa.gov/policy/docs/ssb/v63n1/index.html.

[37] Ibid., p. 6.

[38] 42 U.S.C. § 401(g)(1)(A).

[39] Social Security Administration, *Social Security Administration, Performance and Accountability Report, Fiscal Year 2003*, November 10, 2003, and subsequent editions, http://www.ssa.gov/finance/.

[40] FY2000 data is from the Social Security Advisory Board, *Aspects of Disability Decision Making: Data and Materials*, February 2012, Table 13, p. 18, http://www.ssab.gov /PublicationViewOptions.aspx?ssab_pub=115, while FY2007 and FY2012 data is from the Social Security Administration, *Social Security Administration, Performance and Accountability Report, Fiscal Year 2012*, November 8, 2012, p. 80, http://www.ssa.gov /finance/.

[41] SSDI Annual Report 2011, Table 1, p. 17.

[42] In addition to the incidence and termination rates, the size of the SSDI program is determined by a third factor: the duration of benefit receipt. A beneficiary's length of stay on SSDI is primarily a function of his or her age and diagnosis. Duration of benefit receipt is discussed in the "The Disability Benefits Reform Act of 1984" subsection of the report. For more information on the determinants to program size, see Social Security Administration, *Trends in the Social Security and Supplemental Security Income Disability Programs*, SSA Publication No. 13-11831, August 2006, p. 37, http://www.ssa.gov/policy/docs/chartbooks /disability_trends/index.html (hereinafter cited as "SSA, Trends in SSDI 2006".

[43] 2012 Board of Trustees Report, Table V.C5, p. 131.

[44] 1980 data is from the U.S. General Accounting Office (now called U.S. Government Accountability Office), *Social Security Disability Rolls Keep Growing, While Explanations Remain Elusive*, HEHS-94-34, February 1994, p. 3, http://www.gao.gov/products/HEHS-94-34 (hereinafter cited as "GAO, Disability Rolls Keep Growing 1994"), while 2011 data is from SSDI Annual Report 2011, Table 8, p. 29.

[45] 2012 Board of Trustees Report, p.134.

[46] U.S. Congress, House Committee on Ways and Means, Subcommittee on Social Security, *Johnson Announces Hearing on the Financing Challenges Facing the Social Security*

Disability Insurance Program , Testimony of Stephen C. Goss, Chief Actuary of the Social Security Administration, 113th Cong., 1st sess., March 14, 2013, p. 4, http://waysandmeans.house.gov/uploadedfiles/goss_testimony.pdf (hereinafter cited as "Testimony of Stephen C. Goss 2013").

[47] The 1980 working-age population data is from GAO, Disability Rolls Keep Growing 1994, p. 3, while 2010 working-age population data is from the U.S. Census Bureau, *Annual Estimates of the Resident Population by Sex and Selected Age Groups for the United States: April 1, 2010 to July 1, 2011*, NC-EST2011-02, http://www.census.gov/ popest/data /national/asrh/2011/index.html. Insured worker data computed from the Social Security Administration, *Disability Insured Workers*, http://www.ssa.gov/oact/STATS /table4c2DI.html.

[48] Testimony of Stephen C. Goss, 2013, p. 4. According to the Chief Actuary, the growth in the share of the population insured for disability between 1980 and 2010 increased the number of disabled-worker beneficiaries by 8%.

[49] Tim Zayatz, *Social Security Disability Insurance Program Workers Experience: Actuarial Study No. 114*, Social Security Administration, 1999, Table 4, and subsequent editions, http://www.ssa.gov/oact/NOTES/actstud.html. The disability-exposed population excludes insured workers who receive SSDI benefits, whereas the insured-worker population measure includes them. For more information, see 2012 Board of Trustees Report, p. 125.

[50] Bureau of Labor Statistics, *Labor Force Statistics from the Current Population Survey*, http://data.bls.gov/timeseries/ LNS11300002. The labor force participation rate for women has since fallen to 57.1% as of March 2013.

[51] Social Security Advisory Board, *Aspects of Disability Decision Making: Data and Materials*, February 2012, Table 2a, p. 7, http://www.ssab.gov/PublicationViewOptions.aspx? ssab_pub=115 (hereinafter cited as "SSAB Data and Materials 2012").

[52] Ibid., Table 2b.

[53] Tim Zayatz, *Social Security Disability Insurance Program Workers Experience: Actuarial Study No. 122*, Social Security Administration, 2011, Table 4, http://www.ssa.gov/oact /NOTES/actstud.html. Age adjustment computed using the age distribution of the disability-exposed population in the year 2000.

[54] 2012 Board of Trustees Report, p.133.

[55] Testimony of Stephen C. Goss 2013, pp. 7-8.

[56] 2012 Board of Trustees Report, p.133-134. See also Xuguang (Steve) Guo and John F. Burton, Jr., "The Growth in Applications for Social Security Disability Insurance: A Spillover Effect from Workers' Compensation," *Social Security Bulletin*, vol. 72 no. 3, (August 2012), http://www.ssa.gov/policy/docs/ssb/v72n3/v72n3p69.html (hereinafter cited as "Guo and Burton, Jr. 2012").

[57] Congressional Budget Office, *Policy Options for the Social Security Disability Insurance Program*, 4207, July 2012, p. 7, http://www.cbo.gov/publication/43421 (hereinafter cited as "CBO, Policy Options 2012"). For insured worker data, see Social Security Administration, *Disability Insured Workers*, http://www.ssa.gov/oact/STATS/ table4c2DI.html. See also Mark Duggan and Scott A. Imberman, "Why Are the Disability Rolls Skyrocketing? The Contribution of Population Characteristics, Economic Conditions, and Program Generosity," in *Health at Older Ages: The Causes and Consequences of Declining Disability among the Elderly* , ed. David M. Cutler and David A. Wise, National Bureau of Economic Research (University of Chicago Press, 2009), pp. 342-345, http://www.nber.org/ chapters/c11119 (hereinafter cited as "Duggan and Imberman 2009").

[58] 2012 Board of Trustees Report, pp.125-134. See also CBO, Policy Options 2012, p. 7.

[59] See 20 C.F.R. § 404.1563. For more information on vocational factors, please see *Appendix 2 to Subpart P of Part 404 - Medical-Vocational Guidelines* in 20 C.F.R. § 404.

[60] Tim Zayatz, *Social Security Disability Insurance Program Worker Experience: Actuarial Study No. 122*, Social Security Administration, 2011, Table 3, http://www.ssa.gov/oact /NOTES/actstud.html. The share of benefits awarded to workers aged 15 to 24 decreased as well, from 3.3% in 1986 to 2.5% in 2009.

[61] 2012 Board of Trustees Report, pp.133-134.

[62] David R. Francis, *Why do Death Rates Decline?*, National Bureau of Economic Research, http://www.nber.org/ digest/mar02/w8556.html.

[63] Centers for Disease Control and Prevention, *Deaths: Final Data for 2010*, Table 1, http://www.cdc.gov/nchs/data/ dvs/deaths_2010_release.pdf.

[64] Ibid.

[65] Duggan and Imberman 2009, p. 349.

[66] Nazarov, Z, Lee, C. G. (2012). *Disability Statistics from the Current Population Survey (CPS)*. Ithaca, NY: Cornell University Rehabilitation Research and Training Center on Disability Demographics and Statistics (StatsRRTC). Retrieved February 21, 2013 from www.disabilitystatistics.org. The margin of error for both years is ± 0.2.

[67] David Autor and Mark Duggan, *The Growth in the Social Security Disability Rolls: A Fiscal Crisis Unfolding*, National Bureau of Economic Research, Working Paper no.12436, August 2006, p. 17, http://www.nber.org/papers/ w12436 (hereinafter cited as "Autor and Duggan 2006"). See also Duggan and Imberman 2009.

[68] Duggan and Imberman 2009, p. 354

[69] Disability Statistics, *Frequently Asked Questions: What is the definition of disability?*, Maintained by Cornell University, 2013, http://www.disabilitystatistics.org/faq.cfm#Q3. See also SSA, Trends in SSDI 2006, p. 68.

[70] See Kalman Rupp and David Stapleton, *Determinants of the Growth in the Social Security's Administration's Disability Programs: An Overview*, Social Security Administration, vol. 58, no. 4, 1995, http://www.ssa.gov/policy/ docs/ssb/v58n4/v58n4p43.pdf (hereinafter cited as "Rupp and Stapleton 1995"). See also David H. Autor and Mark G. Duggan, "The Rise in the Disability Rolls and the Decline in Unemployment," *The Quarterly Journal of Economics*, February 2003, pp. 158-205. In addition, see Guo and Burton, Jr. 2012, p. 78.

[71] SSA Annual Statistical Supplement 2012, Table 6.C7. Although there is no official definition of recession, federal agencies such as the Bureau of Economic Analysis (BEA) generally use the definition of recession outlined by the National Bureau of Economic Research (NBER)—a private, non-profit research organization. NBER does not use the often-cited definition of recession as two consecutive quarters of decline in real Gross Domestic Product (GDP). Instead, the organization defines recession as a "significant decline in economic activity spread across the economy, lasting more than a few months, normally visible in real GDP, real income, employment, industrial production, and wholesale-retail sales." For more information, see the National Bureau of Economic Research, *US Business Cycle Expansions and Contractions*, http://www.nber.org/cycles.html.

[72] Duggan and Imberman 2009 p. 355

[73] Kalman Rupp, "Factors Affecting Initial Disability Allowance Rates for the Disability Insurance and Supplemental Security Income Programs: The Role of the Demographic and Diagnostic Composition of Applicants and Local Labor Market Conditions," *Social Security Bulletin*, vol. 72 no. 4, (November 2012), p. 32, http://www.ssa.gov/policy/docs/ ssb/v72n4/v72n4p11.html. Rupp found that an increase in the state unemployment rate is associated with a decrease in the initial allowance rate. The allowance rate is the number of

medical allowances divided by the number of medical decisions. Unlike the award rate (awards divided by applications minus pending claims), the allowance rate does not include technical denials at the initial determination level. Technical denials are issued when a claimant fails to meet the non-disability eligibility requirements (i.e., work history and earnings).

[74] Rupp and Stapleton 1995, p. 56

[75] SSA Annual Statistical Supplement 2012, Table 6.C7.

[76] For more information on how benefits are calculated, see CRS Report R42035, *Social Security Primer*, by Dawn Nuschler.

[77] For more information, see L. Scott Muller, "The Effects of Wage Indexing on Social Security Disability Benefits," *Social Security Bulletin*, vol. 68 no. 3, (December 2008), p. 25, http://www.ssa.gov/policy/docs/ssb/v68n3/ v68n3p1.html (hereinafter cited as "Muller 2008").

[78] CRS Report RL34155, *Income Inequality and the U.S. Tax System*, by Thomas L. Hungerford.

[79] See Autor and Duggan 2006, Table 2. See also Muller 2008, Table 1.

[80] Dana A. Kerr and Bert J. Smoluk, "Macroeconomic Influences on Social Security Disability Insurance Application Rates," *Journal of Insurance Issues*, vol. 34, no. 2 (2011), pp. 112-150, http://econpapers.repec.org/article/wrijournl/ v_3a34_3ay_3a2011_3ai_3a2_3ap_3[a] 112-150.htm. The authors compute the wage gap "by dividing a national labor productivity index produced from data published by the Bureau of Labor Statistics by the annual earnings of workers with only a high school degree." The wage gap measures "the decline in relative earnings power of individuals with only a high school degree."

[81] See Autor and Duggan 2006, as well as Muller 2008. Muller contends that the overall increase in the average replacement rate does not offer low-income workers large incentives to drop out of the labor force and apply for SSDI, especially since changes in replacements rates appear much smaller for low-income earners relative to medium and high-income earners (author's calculations). Autor and Duggan argue that the high-wage replacement of SSDI benefits relative to available compensation makes SSDI enrollment particularly attractive to low-income workers, citing that in 2004, males aged 40 to 64 without a high school degree were five times as likely to receive SSDI benefits relative to males with a college degree (authors' calculations).

[82] Kaiser Family Foundation, *Health Care Costs: A Primer*, Figure 16, May 9, 2012, p. 19, http://www.kff.org/ insurance/7670.cfm. Health insurance premiums are for family premiums based on a family of four.

[83] Carmen DeNavas-Walt, Bernadette D. Proctor, and Jessica C. Smith, *Income, Poverty, and Health Insurance Coverage in the United States: 2010*, Census Bureau, Current Population Reports, P60-239, Table C-1, September 2011, p. 77, http://www.census.gov/prod/2011 pubs/p60-239.pdf. Between 1999 and 2010, the percentage of the population covered by government health insurance increased from 24.2% to 31.0%. However, the overall percentage of the population covered by any health insurance declined during this period from 86.4% to 83.7%.

[84] See Jae Kennedy, Ph.D. and Elizabeth Blodgett, M.H.P.A., *Health Insurance–Motivated Disability Enrollment and the ACA*, The New England Journal of Medicine, September 20, 2012, http://www.nejm.org/doi/full/10.1056/ NEJMp1208212.

[85] For more information on ACA, see CRS Report R41664, *ACA: A Brief Overview of the Law, Implementation, and Legal Challenges*, coordinated by C. Stephen Redhead.

[86] For information on medical considerations, residual functional capacity, and vocational considerations, see 20 C.F.R. § 404.1525, 20 C.F.R. § 404.1545, and 20 C.F.R. § 404.1560, respectively.

[87] For additional information, see Alexander Strand, *Social Security Disability Programs: Assessing the Variation in Allowance Rates*, Social Security Administration, ORES Working Paper no. 98, August 2002, http://www.ssa.gov/ policy/docs/workingpapers/ wp98.html. See also Norma B. Coe et al., *What Explains Variation in SSDI Application Rates?*, Center for Retirement Research at Boston College, WP#2011-23, http://crr.bc.edu/working-papers/whatexplains-state-variation-in-ssdi-application-rates/.

[88] Nicole Maestas, Kathleen J. Mullen, and Alexander Strand, *Does Disability Insurance Receipt Discourage Work? Using Examiner Assignment to Estimate Causual Effects of SSDI Receipt*, RAND Corporation, Working Paper WR853.3, June 2012, p. 23, http://www.rand.org/pubs/working_papers/WR853-3.html (hereinafter cited as "Maestas, Mullen, and Strand 2012").

[89] U.S. Congress, House Ways and Means, Social Security, *Third in a Hearing Series on Securing the Future of the Social Security Disability Insurance Program*, 112th Cong., 2nd sess., March 20, 2012, 112-SS14, Testimony of Nicole Maestas, p. 3, http://waysandmeans. house.gov/uploadedfiles/nicolemaestas_ss_3_20_12s.pdf.

[90] Ibid. Note that although the study found that 23% of applicants could have received a different outcome, there is no guarantee that the applicants would have received a different decision had their cases been assigned to a different DDS examiner.

[91] Maestas, Mullen, and Strand 2012, p. 23.

[92] SSAB Data and Materials 2012, Table 49, p. 54. Dispositions include decisions and dismissals. In FY2010, of the 737,616 dispositions before ALJs, 2,170 were for OASI cases, 232,801 for SSDI-only cases, 200,681 for SSI-only cases, and 301,964 for concurrent SSDI and SSI cases. For more information, see SSA Annual Statistical Supplement 2012, Table 2.F9.

[93] SSAB Data and Materials 2012, Table 7, p. 12.

[94] Social Security Administration, *SSA FY 2012 Budget Justification*, Table 3.20, February 2011, p. 103, http://www.ssa.gov/budget/. Since FY2010, the allowance rate at the hearing level has decreased markedly, declining from 62% in FY2010 to 52% in FY2012. For more information, see Social Security Administration, *SSA FY 2014 Budget Justification*, Table 3.26, April 2013, p. 134, http://www.ssa.gov/budget/FY14Files/2014FJ.pdf.

[95] Maestas, Mullen, and Strand 2012, p. 11.

[96] See Autor and Duggan 2006, p. 20-23.

[97] Kearney 2006, pp. 10-11.

[98] Ibid., p. 14.

[99] Kearney 2006, p. 15.

[100] "Cutoffs for Mentally Ill Bring Moratorium Plea," *The New York Times*, April 9, 1983, http://www.nytimes.com/ 1983/04/10/us/cutoffs-for-mentally-ill-bring-moratorium-plea. html?n= Top%2fReference%2fTimes%20Topics%2fSubjects%2fF%2fFinances.

[101] Kearney 2006, p. 16.

[102] Katharine P. Collins and Anne Erfle, "Social Security Disability Benefits Reform Act of 1984: Legislative History and Summary of Provisions," *Social Security Bulletin*, vol. 48, no. 4, (April 1985), p. 5, http://199.173.224.108/policy/ docs/ssb/v48n4/v48n4p5.pdf.

[103] Kearney 2006, p. 17. See also 20 C.F.R. § 404.1594.

[104] Ibid. For information on the *Listing of Impairments*, please see the Social Security Administration publication *Disability Evaluation Under Social Security*, available at http://www.ssa.gov/disability/professionals/bluebook/. This publication is commonly

referred to as the *SSA Blue Book*. For more information on functional capabilities, please see *Appendix 2 to Subpart P of Part 404 - Medical-Vocational Guidelines* in 20 C.F.R. § 404.

[105] Kearney 2006, p. 17. See also 20 C.F.R. § 404.1523.

[106] Social Security Administration, *A History of the Social Security Disability Programs*, January 1986, http://www.ssa.gov/history/1986dibhistory.html. For more information on the distinction between severe and non-severe impairments, please see Social Security Administration, *DI 22001.015 Severe/Non-Severe Impairment(s)*, July 2012, https://secure.ssa.gov/poms.nsf/lnx/0422001015. See also 20 C.F.R. § 404.1520(c) and 20 C.F.R. § 404.1521.

[107] Most of the growth in mental disorders stems from workers under age 50, while most of the growth in musculoskeletal impairments stems from workers over age 50. For more information, see SSDI Annual Report 2011, Tables 41-42, pp. 109-116.

[108] Autor and Duggan 2006, p. 11.

[109] SSDI Annual Report 2011, Table 40, pp. 103-108.

[110] Kalman Rupp and Charles G. Scott, "Trends in the Characteristics of DI and SSI Disability Awardees and Duration of Program Participation," *Social Security Bulletin*, vol. 59, no. 1, (January 1996), pp. 6-7, http://www.ssa.gov/policy/ docs/ssb/v59n1/index.html (hereinafter cited as "Rupp and Scott 1996"). See also Autor and Duggan 2006, pp.11-12.

[111] Rupp and Scott 1996, Table 1, p. 6. Rupp and Scott examined the age and diagnostic mix of new SSDI cohorts between 1975 and 1993. Recovery, death, and termination rates based on the percent distribution of reasons for completion of first SSDI disability spell by diagnostic group. Musculoskeletal recovery rates are higher for younger individuals (aged 18 to 34). See also John C. Hennessey and Janice M. Dykacz, "A Comparison of the Recovery Termination Rates of Disabled-Worker Beneficiaries Entitled in 1972 and 1985," *Social Security Bulletin*, vol. 56, no. 2, (Summer 1993), pp. 60-61, http://www.ssa.gov/policy/docs /ssb/v56n2/v56n2p58.pdf.

[112] Rupp and Scott 1996, Table 2, p. 7. For a cohort of beneficiaries awarded benefits in 1972, younger beneficiaries (aged 18 to 34) under the diagnostic category "mental disorders" experienced an average duration of benefit receipt of 25.5 years.

[113] For more information, see the National Commission on Social Security Reform, *Report of the National Commission on Social Security Reform*, January 1983, http://www.ssa.gov /history/reports/gspan.html.

[114] See Social Security Administration, *Social Security Amendments of 1983*, http://www.ssa.gov /history/ 1983amend2.html. For more information on changes to the full retirement age, see CRS Report R41962, *Fact Sheet: The Social Security Retirement Age*, by Gary Sidor. For additional information on the graduated increase in the early retirement penalty, see Social Security Administration, *Retirement Planner: Benefits By Year Of Birth*, October 17, 2012, http://www.socialsecurity.gov/retire2/agereduction.htm.

[115] For insured worker data, see Social Security Administration, *Disability Insured Workers*, http://www.ssa.gov/oact/ STATS/table4c2DI.html.

[116] For more information, see U.S. Government Accountability Office, *Raising the Retirement Ages Would Have Implications for Older Workers and SSA Disability Rolls*, GAO-11-125, December 18, 2010, p. 27, http://www.gao.gov/products/GAO-11-125.

[117] CBO, Policy Options 2012, p. 9.

[118] SSA Annual SSDI Report 2011, Table 20, p. 60.

[119] See Norma B. Coe and Kelly Haverstick, *Measuring the Spillover to Disability Insurance Due to the Rise in the Full Retirement Age*, Center for Retirement Research at Boston College,

CRR WP 2010-21, December 2010, p. 9-14, http://crr.bc.edu/working-papers/measuring-the-spillover-to-disability-insurance-due-to-the-rise-in-the-full-retirementage/ (hereinafter cited as "Coe and Haverstick 2010"). In addition, see Mark Duggan, Perry Singleton, and Jae Song, *Aching to Retire? The Rise in the Full Retirement Age and its Impact on the Disability Rolls*, National Bureau of Economic Research, Working Paper 11811, December 2005, http://www.nber.org/papers/w11811 (hereinafter cited as "Duggan, Singleton, and Song 2005").

[120] Ibid. Using aggregate data, Duggan, Singleton, and Song found that the 1983 amendments increased SSDI enrollment 0.58 percentage points for men (aged 45 to 64) and 0.89 percentage points for women (aged 45 to 64) between 1983 and 2005. Using disaggregate data, Coe and Haverstick found that a 1 percentage point decrease in the ratio of retirement to disability benefits resulted in a 0.25 percentage point increase in the application rate for individuals born between 1938 and 1943. However, the researchers found no evidence that the increase in FRA resulted in a rise in the incidence of SSDI receipt among individuals aged 55 to FRA born between 1938 and 1941 (1942 and 1943 cohorts had not reached FRA).

[121] Testimony of Stephen C. Goss 2013, pp. 4-5. Projections based on the Social Security Board of Trustees' 2012 intermediate assumptions.

[122] Ibid.

[123] Ibid., p. 1.

[124] In addition to reducing the prevalence of benefit receipt, there are a number of other reform options for improving the solvency of the DI trust fund. For example, changing the formula for calculating benefits or slowing the growth in COLAs via chained CPI would both abate future program costs (see CBO, Policy Options 2012). Alternatively, raising additional revenue by increasing the taxable earnings base would help to close the gap between program costs and income. For more information on changes to the taxable earnings base, see CRS Report RL33943, *Increasing the Social Security Payroll Tax Base: Options and Effects on Tax Burdens*, by Thomas L. Hungerford and CRS Report RL32896, *Social Security: Raising or Eliminating the Taxable Earnings Base*, by Janemarie Mulvey.

[125] The Social Security Advisory Board is an independent board tasked with advising the Commissioner of Social Security on issues related to OASDI and SSI. For more information, see 42 U.S.C. § 903.

[126] Maestas, Mullen, and Strand 2012, p. 22. Maestas, Mullen, and Strand found that the employment of marginal program entrants would have been on average 28 percentage points higher two years after the initial determination had they not received SSDI. This figure drops to 16 percentage points four years after the initial determination. However, these estimations reflect economic and labor market conditions between 2005 and 2006, and therefore may not hold during instances of high unemployment such as the December 2007 to June 2009 recession.

[127] Ibid., p. 5.

[128] CBO, Policy Options 2012.

[129] See 20 C.F.R. § 404.130(b)(2).

[130] CRS Report (Archived), *Social Security: Summary of Major Changes in the Cash Benefits Program*, May 18, 2000, available at http://www.ssa.gov/history/reports/crsleghist2.html.

[131] CBO, Policy Options 2012, p. 18.

[132] Unemployment refers to all individuals aged 16 and over who do not have a job, have actively looked for work in the prior four weeks, and are currently available for work. Individuals out of the labor force are currently not working and not actively looking for a job.

[133] Julie L. Hotchkiss, M. Melinda Pitts, and Fernando Rios-Avila, *A Closer Look at Nonparticipants During and After the Great Recession*, Federal Reserve Bank, Working Paper 2012-10, August 2012, p. 6, http://www.frbatlanta.org/ pubs/wp/12_10.cfm.

[134] In *Collier v. Barnhart*, Claire Collier, a wife and mother suffering from amyotrophic lateral sclerosis (ALS; also known as Lou Gehrig's disease), filed suit in U.S. district court in 2005 against the Commissioner of Social Security, arguing that the recency-of-work requirement (or 20/40 rule) violated the equal protection component of the Due Process Clause of the Fifth Amendment. Although Mrs. Collier satisfied the quarters of coverage requirement for her age, she did not meet the 20/40 rule due to her six years as a stay-at-home mother. Mrs. Collier argued that the 20/40 rule discriminates against stay-at-home mothers who have made "significant contributions" to SSDI and Medicare. The district court found that the 20/40 rule did not violate equal protection or due process and ultimately granted the Commissioner's motion for summary judgment. For more information, see Sarah E. Hoffman, "Falling Through the Cracks: How the 20/40 Rule Discriminates Against Women Seeking Social Security Disability Insurance Benefits and What Congress Can Do About It," *Penn State Law Review*, vol. 113, no. 2 (2008).

[135] Social Security Administration, *DI 25001.001 Medical-Vocational Quick Reference Guide*, May 2012, https://secure.ssa.gov/poms.nsf/lnx/0425001001. Although this CRS report defines older workers as individuals aged 45 and older, SSA categories individuals under the age of 50 as "younger individuals." For more information, see *Appendix 2 to Subpart P of Part 404 - Medical-Vocational Guidelines* in 20 C.F.R. § 404.

[136] CBO, Policy Options 2012, p. 18. Adjusting the age ranges of vocational factors would have also decreased participation in Medicare and thus reduced Medicare outlays.

[137] For more information on other potential income supports for SSDI applicants, see CRS Report RS22220, *Social Security Disability Insurance (SSDI): The Five-Month Waiting Period for Benefits*, by Umar Moulta-Ali. Adjusting the age ranges for vocational factors would have increased participation in and outlays to SSI and Medicaid, although CBO did not provide specific estimates. For more information see, CBO, Policy Options 2012, p. 18.

[138] For more information, see Social Security Administration, "Age as a Factor in Evaluating Disability," 70 *Federal Register* 67104, November 4, 2005.

[139] See Social Security Administration, "Age as a Factor in Evaluating Disability," 74 *Federal Register* 21563, May 8, 2009.

[140] See 20 C.F.R. § 404.900(b), 20 C.F.R. § 416.1400(b), and 20 C.F.R. § 405.1(c).

[141] U.S. Congress, House Committee on Ways and Means, Subcommittee on Social Security, *Chairman Johnson Announces the Fourth in a Hearing Series on Securing the Future of the Social Security Disability Insurance Program*, Testimony of Ethel Zelenske, 112th Cong., 2nd sess., June 27, 2012, http://waysandmeans.house.gov/uploadedfiles/ zelenske_testimony.pdf.

[142] See Social Security Advisory Board, *Charting the Future of Social Security's Disability Programs: The Need for Fundamental Change*, January 2001, p. 19, http://www.ssab.gov/Publications/Disability/disabilitywhitepap.pdf (hereinafter cited as "SSAB Fundamental Change 2001"). See also U.S. Congress, House Committee on Ways and Means, Subcommittee on Social Security, *Chairman Johnson Announces the Fourth in a Hearing Series on Securing the Future of the Social Security Disability Insurance Program* , Testimony of the Honorable D. Randall Frye, 112th Cong., 2nd sess., June 27, 2012 (hereinafter cited as "Testimony of the Honorable D. Randall Frye 2012").

[143] Testimony of the Honorable D. Randall Frye 2012, p. 5.

[144] Ibid. See also SSAB Fundamental Change 2001, p. 19.

[145] SSAB Fundamental Change 2001, p. 19.

[146] SSA's Office of the Inspector General, *Identifying and Monitoring Risk Factors at Hearing Offices*, Audit Report: A-12-12-11289, January 2013, p. 7, http://oig.ssa.gov/audits-and-investigations/audit-reports/A-12-12-11289.

[147] Ibid.

[148] Social Security Advisory Board, *Filing for Social Security Disability Benefits: What Impact Does Professional Representation Have on the Process at the Initial Level*, September 2012, p. 6, footnote 9, http://www.ssab.gov/ Reports/Third-Party-2012-Full.pdf.

[149] Salling v. Bowen, 641 F. Supp. 1046 (W.D. Va. 1986). See also Frank Bloch, Jeffrey Lubbers, and Paul Verkuil, *Introducing Nonadversarial Government Representatives to Improve the Record of Decision in Social Security Disability Adjudications*, Social Security Advisory Board, 2003, http://www.ssab.gov/documents/Bloch-LubbersVerkuil.pdf.

[150] SSA's demonstration authority expired in 2005. For more information, see CRS Report RL33585, *Social Security Disability Insurance (SSDI) Demonstration Projects*, by Scott Szymendera.

[151] If the evidence from a claimant's medical sources is insufficient to make a disability determination, DDS examiners can arrange for a consultative examination of the claimant to obtain the necessary information. For more information, see Social Security Administration, *Consultative Examinations: A Guide for Health Professionals*, Part III - Consultative Examination Guidelines, March 28, 2013, http://www.ssa.gov/disability/professionals /greenbook/ceguidelines.htm. This publication is commonly referred to as the *SSA Green Book*. See also Social Security Administration, *DI 22510.001 General – Consultative Examination (CE)*, November 30, 2012, https://secure.ssa.gov/ poms.nsf/lnx/0422510001.

[152] For information on the *Listing of Impairments*, please see the Social Security Administration publication *Disability Evaluation Under Social Security*, available at http://www.ssa.gov/disability/professionals/bluebook/. This publication is commonly referred to as the *SSA Blue Book*. For additional information, see the U.S. Government Accountability Office, *Modernizing SSA Disability Programs: Progress Made, but Key Efforts Warrant More Management Focus*, GAO-12-420, June 19, 2012, p. 3, http://www.gao.gov/products/GAO-12-420 (hereinafter cited as "GAO, Modernizing SSA Disability Programs 2012").

[153] For more information, see Social Security Administration, *DI 34001.001 Listing of Impairments—Purpose, Parts and Use*, POMS, February 26, 2013, https://secure.ssa.gov/poms.nsf/lnx/0434001001.

[154] Social Security Advisory Board, *The Social Security Definition of Disability*, October 2003, p. 4, http://www.ssab.gov/documents/SocialSecurityDefinitionOfDisability.pdf (hereinafter cited as "SSAB Definition of Disability 2003").

[155] SSAB Data and Materials 2012, Table 40, p. 45.

[156] Ibid. Figures may not equal 100% due to rounding.

[157] SSA's Office of the Inspector General, *The Social Security Administration's Listing of Impairments*, A-01-08- 18023, March 27, 2009, p. 4, http://oig.ssa.gov/social-security-administrations-listing-impairments.

[158] U.S. General Accounting Office, *High Risk Series: An Update*, GAO-03-119, January 1, 2003, pp. 20-21, http://www.gao.gov/products/GAO-03-119. GAO designates certain federal programs as "high risk" in order to draw attention to issues related to efficiency, effectiveness, and accountability.

[159] SSAB Definition of Disability 2003, p. 4.

[160] GAO, Modernizing SSA Disability Programs 2012, p. 5.

[161] Ibid., pp. 5-8. In 2010, SSA set a five-year cycle for updating listings following a comprehensive review.

[162] U.S. Congress, House Committee on Appropriations, Subcommittee on Labor, Health and Human Services, Education, and Related Agencies, *Addressing Social Security Administration's Management Challenges in a Fiscally Constrained Environment* , Testimony of Carolyn Colvin, Acting Commissioner of the Social Security Administration, 113th Cong., 1st sess., March 14, 2013, p. 7, http://appropriations.house.gov/uploadedfiles /hhrg-113-ap07-wstatecolvinc-20130314.pdf (hereinafter cited as "Testimony of Carolyn Colvin 2013").

[163] SSA is still in the process of completing comprehensive revisions to the following adult body systems: mental disorders, hematological disorders, the respiratory system, and neurological disorders. Information based on personal communication with a SSA official, March 28, 2013.

[164] GAO, Modernizing SSA Disability Programs 2012 p. 11. According to GAO, SSA published a limited update to the mental disorders listing in 2000.

[165] Ibid., p. 12.

[166] Testimony of Carolyn Colvin 2013, p. 7.

[167] U.S. Congress, House Committee on Ways and Means, Subcommittee on Social Security, *Chairman Johnson Announces the Third in a Hearing Series on Securing the Future of the Social Security Disability Insurance Program* , Testimony of Michael J. Astrue, Commissioner of the Social Security Administration, 112th Cong., 2nd sess., March 20, 2012, http://www.ssa.gov/legislation/testimony_032012.html. See also GAO, Modernizing SSA Disability Programs 2012, p. 4.

[168] GAO, Modernizing SSA Disability Programs 2012, p. 6. DOT received a minor update in 1991, albeit for only about 20% of all occupations covered in the database.

[169] Ibid., p. 14.

[170] U.S. Congress, Senate Committee on Homeland Security and Governmental Affairs, Permanent Subcommittee on Investigations, *Social Security Disability Programs: Improving the Quality of Benefit Award Decisions*, Minority Staff Report, 112th Cong., 2nd sess., September 13, 2012, p. 5, http://www.hsgac.senate.gov/subcommittees/investigations/ hearings/social-security-administrations-disability-programs.

[171] Social Security Administration, *Occupational Information System Project*, March 18, 2013, http://www.ssa.gov/ disabilityresearch/occupational_info_systems.html (hereinafter cited as "OIS Project 2013").

[172] Ibid.

[173] Social Security Administration, *Social Security Administration (SSA) Service Delivery Plan*, February 20, 2013, p. 19, http://www.ssa.gov/open/SDP/SDP_022013.pdf.

[174] Robert Pfaff, *Prior SSA Work to Address the DOT Concerns*, Social Security Administration, Occupational Information Development Advisory Panel, February 24, 2009, slide 2, http://www.socialsecurity.gov/oidap/ Documents/Social%20Security%20Administration.%20Prior%20SSA%20Work%20to%20 Address%20th.pdf.

[175] U.S. Congress, House Committee on Ways and Means, Subcommittee on Social Security, *Chairman Johnson Announces Hearing on the Challenges of Achieving Fair and Consistent Disability Decisions*, Testimony of Kathy Ruffing, Senior Fellow at the Center on Budget and Policy Priorities, 113th Cong., 1st sess., March 20, 2013, http://waysandmeans.house. gov/uploadedfiles/ruffing_testimony32013.pdf (hereinafter cited s "Testimony of Kathy Ruffing 2013").

[176] Richard W. Johnson, Gordon B.T. Mermin, and Matthew Resseger, *Employment at Older Ages and the Changing Nature of Work*, The AARP Public Policy Institute, November 2007, p. 1, http://www.urban.org/UploadedPDF/ 1001154_older_ages.pdf.

[177] Social Security Administration, *SSA FY 2013 Budget Justification*, February 2012, p. 2, http://www.ssa.gov/budget/.

[178] Social Security Administration, *Annual Report of Continuing Disability Reviews*, May 1, 2012, p. 2, http://ssa.gov/ legislation/FY%202010%20CDR%20Report.pdf. Figures reflect CDRs performed under SSA's central release system, as well as CDR's conducted outside SSA's central release process.

[179] Ibid., p. 5. Figure reflects cases processed only under SSA's central release system. In FY2010, CDRs conducted under SSA's central release system resulted in 78,433 initial cessations and 1,945 initial terminations due to FTC.

[180] Ibid. Projected savings reflect the present value of future benefits for OASDI, SSI, Medicare, and Medicaid as of September 30, 2010. Projected savings do not take into account the lifetime benefits of terminated beneficiaries processed outside SSA's central release system. The $9.3 to $1.0 savings-to-cost ratio is calculated by dividing OCAct's projected future savings of more than $3.5 billion by the $381 million spent on periodic CDRs in FY2010.

[181] U.S. Congress, House Committee on Ways and Means, Subcommittee on Social Security, *Chairman Johnson Announces the Second in a Hearing Series on Securing the Future of the Social Security Disability Insurance Program*, Testimony of Carolyn Colvin, Deputy Commissioner of the Social Security Administration, 112th Cong., 2nd sess., January 24, 2012, http://www.ssa.gov/legislation/testimony_012412.html.

[182] SSA's Office of the Inspector General, *Full Medical Continuing Disability Reviews*, March 30, 2010, p. 2, http://oig.ssa.gov/full-medical-continuing-disability-reviews.

[183] Ibid., C-3. Estimates assume a cessation rate of between 6% and 12%. Estimated savings reflect avoided SSI and SSDI payments between CY2005 and CY2010 and do not include payments made under Medicare or Medicaid.

[184] Social Security Administration, *Social Security Administration, Performance and Accountability Report, Fiscal Year2012*, November 8, 2012, p. 184, http://www.ssa.gov /finance/(hereinafter cited as "SSA FY2012 Performance and Accountability").

[185] U.S. Congress, House Committee on Ways and Means, Subcommittee on Social Security, Chairman Johnson Announces the First in a Hearing Series on Securing the Future of the Social Security Disability Insurance Program , Statement for the Record from the Consortium for Citizens with Disabilities, 112th Cong., 1st sess., December 2, 2011, Serial 112–SS11 (Washington: GPO, 2012). See also Testimony of Kathy Ruffing 2013, p. 15. Moreover, see Office of Management and Budget, Fiscal Year 2014 Budget of the U.S. Government, 2013, p. 138, http://www.whitehouse.gov/sites/default/files/omb /budget/ fy2014/assets/budget.pdf.

[186] For more information on SSA budgetary issues, see CRS Report R41716, *Social Security Administration (SSA): Budget Issues*, by Scott Szymendera. SSI redeterminations are periodic reviews to ensure that beneficiaries continually meet SSI eligibility requirements. For additional information on SSI redeterminations, see 20 C.F.R. § 416.204.

[187] Testimony of Carolyn Colvin 2013, pp. 9-10. SSA performed approximately 443,000 full medical CDRs in FY2012. Estimated savings based on FY2013 budget assumptions.

[188] Office of Management and Budget, *Analytical Perspectives, Budget of the United States Government, Fiscal Year 2014*, 2013, pp. 148-149, http://www.whitehouse.gov/sites/default /files/omb/budget/fy2014/assets/spec.pdf.

[189] Ibid.

[190] As of September 2012, only Nevada, New York, Oregon, and Washington were still furloughing DDS employees. See SSA FY2012 Performance and Accountability, p. 184. For more information on SSA workforce issues, see CRS Report R40207, *Social Security Administration: Workload and Related Issues*, by Scott Szymendera.

[191] The SSA's Office of the Inspector General, *The Social Security Administration's Response to State Furloughs Impacting its Disability Programs*, A-01-11-11116, March 22, 2011, p. 6, http://oig.ssa.gov/social-securityadministration%3Fs-response-state-furloughs-impacting-its-disability-programs. See also SSA FY2012 Performance and Accountability, p. 184.

[192] SSA FY2012 Performance and Accountability, p. 184.

[193] U.S. Congress, Senate Committee on Finance, *The Social Security Administration: Is it Meeting its Responsibilities to Save Taxpayer Dollars and Serve the Public?*, Testimony of Michael Astrue, Commissioner of SSA, 112th Cong., 2nd sess., May 17, 2012, http://www.ssa.gov/legislation/testimony_051712.html.

[194] SSA FY2012 Performance and Accountability, p. 184.

[195] U.S. Congress, House Committee on Ways and Means, Subcommittees on Income Security and Family Support and Social Security, *Hearing on Disability Backlogs and Related Service Delivery Issues*, 111th Cong., 1st sess., March 24, 2009, p. 10, http://www.gao.gov/products/GAO-09-511T.

[196] Ibid.

[197] In 2013, SSA considers any month in which the participant's earnings exceed $750 a trial work month. Upon completion of the TWP, the participant may enter a 36-month Extended Period of Eligibility (EPE), during which the participant receives cash benefits only if earnings are below SGA. The EPE is also known as the re-entitlement period. The first three months of the EPE are a grace period, during which SSA pays benefits regardless of the amount of monthly earnings. For more information, see 20 C.F.R. § 404.1592 and 404.1592a. For information on monthly TWP amounts, see Social Security Administration, *Trial Work Period*, October 16, 2012, http://www.ssa.gov/oact/cola/ twp.html.

[198] SSDI Annual Report 2011, Table 57, p. 137. Some longitudinal studies indicate slightly higher return-to-work rates relative to the cross-sectional statistic published in SSA's Annual Statistical Report. One longitudinal study found that of a cohort of beneficiaries examined between 1996 and 2006, 6.5% had their benefits suspended for earnings above SGA in at least 1 month and 3.7% had their benefits eventually terminated due to work. For more information, see Su Liu and David C. Stapleton, "Longitudinal Statistics on Work Activity and Use of Employment Supports for New Social Security Disability Insurance Beneficiaries," *Social Security Bulletin*, vol. 71 no. 3, (August 2011), p. 35, http://www.ssa.gov/policy/docs/ssb/v71n3/v71n3p35.html.

[199] For more information on work incentives, see Social Security Administration, *The Red Book - A Guide to Work Incentives*, SSA Publication No. 64-030, http://ssa.gov/redbook/.

[200] For more information on the Ticket to Work program, see CRS Report R41934, *Ticket to Work and Self-Sufficiency Program: Overview and Current Issues*, by Umar Moulta-Ali (hereinafter cited as "CRS Report R41934").

[201] Gina A. Livermore and Allison Roche, "Longitudinal Outcomes of an Early Cohort of Ticket to Work Participants," *Social Security Bulletin*, vol. 71, no. 3, (August 2011), pp. 105-116, http://www.ssa.gov/policy/docs/ssb/v71n3/ v71n3p105.html. According to the study, in 2004, 32% of Ticket to Work participants were employed compared with only 9% of all SSDI and SSI beneficiaries. For more information on the number of tickets "in use," see CRS Report R41934.

[202] U.S. Government Accountability Office, *Ticket to Work Participation Has Increased, but Additional Oversight Needed*, GAO-11-324, May 6, 2011, p. 11, http://www.gao.gov /products/GAO-11-324.

[203] Bonnie O'Day and David Stapleton, *The United Kingdom Pathways to Work Program: A Path to Employment?*, Mathematica Policy Research, Inc., Number 08-02, September 2008, http://www.mathematica-mpr.com/publications/ PDFs/pathways_disbrief2.pdf (hereinafter cited as "O'Day and Stapleton 2008").

[204] Ibid., p. 1.

[205] The agency could exempt beneficiaries with a low probability of recovery from the counseling requirement, since they are less likely to return to work compared to other beneficiaries.

[206] O'Day and Stapleton 2008. In 2011, the U.K. government replaced Pathways to Work with the Work Programme, which is a consolidation of all U.K. welfare-to-work programs. For more information, see U.K. National Audit Office, *Department of Work and Pensions: The Introduction of the Work Programme*, Report by the Comptroller and Auditor General, HC 1701 Session 2010–2012, January 24, 2012, http://www.official-documents.gov.uk /document/hc1012/ hc17/1701/1701.pdf.

[207] New beneficiaries with a low probability of recovery or high likelihood of returning to work without additional assistance were required to attend only one WFI. Existing beneficiaries were required to attend three WFI unless given exemption. For more information, see Stuart Adam et al., *A Cost-Benefit Analysis of Pathways to Work for New and Repeat Incapacity Benefits Claims*, U.K. Department of Work and Pensions, Research Report No 498, 2008, p. 8, http://discovery.ucl.ac.uk/17916/1/17916.pdf.

[208] Ibid., pp. 131-132. The savings-to-cost ratio to the government (Exchequer) was £1.51 ($2.75) to £1.00 ($1.82). Cost estimates pertain to the 12-month period between April 2005 and March 2006. U.S. dollar amounts reflect the 2005 annual average exchange rate from The World Bank, *Official exchange rate (LCU per US$, period average)*, http://data.worldbank.org/indicator/PA.NUS.FCRF?page=1.

[209] Helen Bewley, Richard Dorsett, and Getinet Haile, *The Impact of Pathways to Work*, U.K. Department for Work and Pensions, Research Report No 435, 2007, p. 2, http://research.dwp.gov.uk/asd/asd5/rports2007-2008/rrep435.pdf. The employment rate of the control group was 29.7%.

[210] Prior to 2006, WIPA was known as the Benefits Planning Assistance and Outreach (BPAO) program. Although authorization for WIPA and PABSS expired on June 30, 2012 and September 30, 2012, respectively, the Consolidated and Further Continuing Appropriations Act, 2013 (P.L. 113-6) appropriated money to both programs through the rest of FY2013. For more information, see CRS Report R41934.

[211] Gina Livermore, Sarah Prenovitz, and Jody Schimmel, *Employment-Related Outcomes of a Recent Cohort of Work Incentives Planning and Assistance (WIPA) Program Enrollees*, Mathematica Policy, Inc., Final Report, September 19, 2011, p. 51, http://www.ssa.gov /disabilityresearch/documents/WIPA%20Cohort%20September%202011.pdf.

[212] O'Day and Stapleton 2008, p. 3.

[213] Ibid.

[214] For more information, see footnote 197.

[215] Jody Schimmel, David C. Stapleton, and Jae G. Song, "How Common is "Parking" among Social Security Disability Insurance Beneficiaries? Evidence from the 1999 Change in the Earnings Level of Substantial Gainful Activity," *Social Security Bulletin*, vol. 71 no. 4, (November 2011), p. 77, http://www.ssa.gov/policy/docs/ssb/v71n4/ v71n4p77.html.

[216] Gina A. Livermore and Allison Roche, "Longitudinal Outcomes of an Early Cohort of Ticket to Work Participants," *Social Security Bulletin*, vol. 71, no. 3, (August 2011), p. 120, Table 11, http://www.ssa.gov/policy/docs/ssb/v71n3/ v71n3p105.html.

[217] For more information, see Willem Van Zandweghe, "Interpreting the Recent Decline in Labor Force Participation," *Federal Reserve Bank of Kansas City Economic Review*, First Quarter 2012, pp. 28-29, http://www.kc.frb.org/publicat/ econrev/pdf/12q1VanZandweghe.pdf.

[218] U.S. Congress, House Committee on Ways and Means, Subcommittee on Social Security, *Chairman Johnson Announces the Fifth in a Hearing Series on Securing the Future of the Social Security Disability Insurance Program* , Testimony of Marty Ford, Director of Public Policy, The Arc of the United States, on behalf of the Consortium for Citizens with Disabilities Social Security Task Force, 112th Cong., 2nd sess., September 14, 2012, p. 5, http://waysandmeans.house.gov/uploadedfiles/ford_testimony_ss914.pdf.

[219] 20 C.F.R. § 416.1112(c)(5) and (7). For more information on SSI, see CRS Report 94-486, *Supplemental Security Income (SSI)*, by Umar Moulta-Ali.

[220] David Wittenburg et al., *BOND Implementation and Evaluation: BOND Stage 1 Early Assessment Report*, Abt Associates Inc. and Mathematica Policy, Inc., Submitted to the Social Security Administration, Deliverable 24.1, May 17, 2012, p. 1, http://www.ssa.gov/disabilityresearch/offsetnational.htm.

[221] David Stapleton et al., *BOND Implementation and Evaluation: BOND Final Design Report*, Abt Associates Inc. and Mathematica Policy, Inc., submitted to the Social Security Administration, Deliverable 2.2, December 3, 2010, p. 6, http://www.ssa.gov/disability research/offsetnational.htm (hereinafter cited as "BOND Final Design Report 2010").

[222] To determine the offset amount, SSA initiates a work CDR of a participant's earnings. Similar to a medical CDR, a work CDR allows SSA to determine whether a beneficiary meets SSDI eligibility criteria regarding earnings. Although BOND participants are exempt from termination due to earnings above SGA, they are still subject to periodic medical CDRs. For more information, see Security Administration, *DI 60099.040 Benefit Offset National Demonstration (BOND) Offset*, January 18, 2012, https://secure.ssa.gov/poms.nsf/lnx/ 0460099040.

[223] BOND Final Design Report 2010, p. 19.

[224] Social Security Administration, *Annual Report on Section 234 Demonstration Projects, May 2011*, May 2011, pp. 4- 5, http://www.ssa.gov/disabilityresearch/newsarchive/2011 news.htm.

[225] U.S. Congress, House Committee on Ways and Means, Subcommittee on Social Security, *Chairman Johnson Announces the Fifth in a Hearing Series on Securing the Future of the Social Security Disability Insurance Program*, Testimony of Richard Burkhauser, Ph.D, 112th Cong., 2nd sess., September 14, 2012, http://waysandmeans.house.gov/ uploadedfiles/burkhauser_testimony_ss914.pdf (hereinafter cited as "Burkhauser Testimony 2012").

[226] Under ADA, "reasonable accommodation" is defined as making existing facilities readily accessible to and usable by individuals with disabilities, and job restructuring, part-time or modified work schedules, reassignment to a vacant position, acquisition or modification of equipment or devices, adjustment of examinations or training materials or policies, provision of qualified readers or interpreters or other similar accommodations. See 42 U.S.C. §12111(9). For more information, see CRS Report 98-921, *The Americans with Disabilities Act (ADA): Statutory Language and Recent Issues*, by Cynthia Brougher.

[227] David C. Stapleton, *Issue Brief: Bending the Employment, Income, and Cost Curves for People with Disabilities*, Mathematica Policy, Inc., Number 11- 01, April 2011, p. 2,

http://www.mathematica-mpr.com/publications/PDFs/ disability/disability_bendemploy_ib.pdf (hereinafter cited as "Stapleton Issue Brief 2011"). Insurance premium determination systems and methodologies vary by state. Workers' compensation provides medical benefits and a partial wage replacement to insured workers whose impairment or condition stems from their employment. Unemployment insurance provides a partial wage replacement to insured workers who become involuntarily unemployed.

[228] Ibid., p. 3. See also Richard V. Burkhauser, Mary C. Daly, and Philip R. de Jong, *Curing the Dutch Disease: Lessons for United States Disability Policy*, University of Michigan Retirement Research Center, Working Paper 2008- 188, September 2008, http://www.mrrc.isr.umich.edu/publications/Papers/pdf/wp188.pdf (hereinafter cited as "Burkhauser, Daly, and de Jong 2008").

[229] SSDI and Medicare's Hospital Insurance (HI; also known as Part A) are financed primarily through the Federal Insurance Contributions Act (FICA) payroll tax and the Self-Employment Contributions Act (SECA) tax, to which all workers and employers in covered occupations (including military personnel) and self-employed individuals contribute. In 2013, the total payroll tax rate is 15.3% on earnings split equally between employees and employers. The SSDI portion of the payroll tax is 1.8% (0.9% each per employee and employer) up to a taxable maximum of $113,700 in 2013.The HI portion of the payroll tax is 2.9% (1.45% each per employee and employer) on all earnings subject to the tax. For more information on OASDI payroll taxes, see CRS Report R41648, *Social Security: Temporary Payroll Tax Reduction*, by Dawn Nuschler. For more information on Medicare's HI portion of the payroll tax, see CRS Report R41436, *Medicare Financing*, by Patricia A. Davis.

[230] Philip R. de Jong, *Recent changes in Dutch disability policy*, Aarts de Jong Wilms Goudriaan Public Economics (APE), September 2008.

[231] Pierre Koning, *Estimating the impact of experience rating on the inflow into disability insurance in the Netherlands*, CBP Netherlands Bureau of Economic Policy Analysis, CPB Discussion Paper no 37, August 2004, http://www.cpb.nl/ en/publication/estimating-impact-experience-rating-inflow-disability-insurance-netherlands. The study found the ex post (after-the-fact) effect of having to pay a premium rate in a given year due to experience rating induced Dutch employers to invest more in preventative services, amounting to a 15% reduction in the inflow of workers into the state DI system after one year.

[232] Burkhauser Testimony 2012. According to Burkhauser, the decline in the Dutch DI prevalence rate stems from numerous reforms instituted over the past 15 years. Because of a series of reforms that began in 2006, Dutch employers now pay a uniform rate for all permanent disability benefits (IVA); however, employers pay experienced-rated premiums on partial disability benefits (WGA) via the state system. Although Dutch firms may opt out of the state system and purchase private insurance, many private DI insurance pools are experienced rated. For more information, see Organization for Economic Co-operation (OECD), *Sickness and Disability Schemes in the Netherlands*, November 2007, http://www.oecd.org/social/soc/41429917.pdf.

[233] David H. Autor, *The Unsustainable Rise of the Disability Rolls in the United States: Causes, Consequences, and Policy Options*, National Bureau of Economic Research, NBER Working Paper No. 17697, December 2011, p. 15, http://www.nber.org/papers/w17697 (hereinafter cited as "Autor NBER Working Paper 2011").

[234] Stapleton Issue Brief 2011, p. 3.

[235] David C. Stapleton et al., "Income Security for Workers: A Stressed Support System in Need of Innovation," *Journal of Disability Policy Studies*, June 20, 2008, p. 11 (hereinafter cited as "Stapleton et al. Income Security for Workers 2008").

[236] Employers may be unable to shift increased labor costs onto employees due to a lower bound restraint such as the minimum wage.

[237] Stapleton Issue Brief 2011, p. 3. Stapleton would offset the reduced compensation with an expansion of the Earned Income Tax Credit (EITC) in order to bolster the after-tax income of low-wage workers. For more information on the EITC, see CRS Report RL31768, *The Earned Income Tax Credit (EITC): An Overview*, by Christine Scott.

[238] CBO, Policy Options 2012, p. 28.

[239] Autor NBER Working Paper 2011, pp. 15-17.

[240] For more information, see the "Changes in the Economic Incentives to Apply for SSDI" section of the report.

[241] Autor NBER Working Paper 2011, p. 16. Moral hazard refers to the tendency for individuals to engage in risky behavior when they are not fully exposed to the consequences of their actions.

[242] Bureau of Labor Statistics, *Insurance benefits: Access, participation, and take-up rates*, Table 16, March 2012, http://www.bls.gov/ncs/ebs/benefits/2012/ownership/private/table12a.htm.

[243] In March 2012, the median duration of benefit receipt on short-term PDI for all workers in private industry was 26 weeks. For more information, see Bureau of Labor Statistics, *Short-term disability plans: Duration of benefits*, Table 25, March 2012, http://www.bls.gov/ncs /ebs/benefits/2012/ownership/private/table35a.htm.

[244] In December 2012, employee health insurance cost employers in private industry $2.23 per-hour worked, whereas employee short-term disability insurance cost $0.05 and long-term disability insurance cost $0.04 per-hour worked. For more information, see Bureau of Labor and Statistics, *Private industry, by major occupational group and bargaining status*, Table 5, December 2012, http://www.bls.gov/news.release/ecec.t05.htm.

[245] In March 2012, 19% of short-term PDI plans sponsored by employers in private industry required employee contributions, whereas 8% of long-term PDI plans had such a requirement. For more information, see Bureau of Labor Statistics, *Employee Benefit Survey: Tables Organized by Benefit*, March 2012, http://www.bls.gov/ncs/ebs/benefits/ 2012/benefits.htm#life.

[246] David H. Autor and Mark Duggan, *Supporting Work: A Proposal for Modernizing the U.S. Disability Insurance System*, The Center for American Progress and The Hamilton Project, http://www.brookings.edu/research/papers/2010/ 12/disability-insurance-autor (hereinafter cited as "Autor and Duggan 2010"). See also Burkhauser, Daly, and de Jong 2008.

[247] See Norma B. Coe et al., *What Explains Variation in SSDI Application Rates?*, Center for Retirement Research at Boston College, WP#2011-23, http://crr.bc.edu/working-papers/what-explains-state-variation-in-ssdi-application-rates/. The authors found that state-mandated temporary disability insurance (TDI) has a small negative effect on overall SSDI applications.

[248] Burkhauser, Daly, and de Jong 2008.

[249] Stapleton et al. Income Security for Workers 2008, p. 11.

[250] CRS Report RL34088, *Leave Benefits in the United States*, by Linda Levine. TDI typically provides partial compensation due to non-occupational disability for approximately 26 to 52 weeks. For more information, see Social Security Administration, *Social Security Programs in the United States*, No. 13-11758, July 1997, p. 46, http://www.SSA .gov/policy/docs/progdesc/sspus/.

[251] Organization for Economic Co-operation and Development, *New Ways of Addressing Partial Work Capacity*, April 2007, pp. 10-11, http://www.oecd.org/social/soc/38509814.pdf.

[252] Autor and Duggan 2010, p. 6.

[253] Ibid., p. 7. Under this proposal, insurance premiums would be experienced rated for firms with 50 or more full-time equivalent employees, whereas smaller firms would have their premiums determined based on differentiated rates by industry.

[254] Ibid., p. 23. Unemployed workers would receive a replacement wage at their state UI rate; however, in order to protect employers from the so-called "double indemnity" of paying higher experienced-rated premiums for both UI and PDI, unemployed workers would be unable to claim both UI and PDI benefits simultaneously.

[255] Internal Revenue Service, *Tax Benefits for Businesses Who Have Employees with Disabilities*, September 24, 2012, http://www.irs.gov/Businesses/Small-Businesses-&-Self-Employed /Tax-Benefits-for-Businesses-Who-HaveEmployees-with-Disabilities. To offset the cost of workplace accommodation, the federal government provides employers with tax credits under the Disabled Access Credit and the Barrier Removal Tax Deduction. In addition, the federal government offers the Work Opportunity Tax Credit to employers who hire members of certain targeted groups, including workers with disabilities.

[256] U.S. General Accounting Office, *Incentives to Employ Workers with Disabilities Receive Limited Use and Have an Uncertain Impact*, GAO-03-39, December 11, 2002, http://www.gao.gov/products/GAO-03-39.

[257] For more information on how the employer penalties work under ACA, see CRS Report R41159, *Potential Employer Penalties Under the Patient Protection and Affordable Care Act (ACA)*, by Janemarie Mulvey.

In: Social Security Disability Insurance
Editor: Harvey Daniels
ISBN: 978-1-62948-776-2

Chapter 2

PRIMER ON DISABILITY BENEFITS: SOCIAL SECURITY DISABILITY INSURANCE (SSDI) AND SUPPLEMENTAL SECURITY INCOME (SSI)*

Umar Moulta-Ali

SUMMARY

In general, the goal of disability insurance is to replace a portion of a worker's income should illness or disability prevent him or her from working. Individuals may receive disability benefits from either federal or state governments, or from private insurers. This report presents information on two components of federal disability benefits, those provided through the Social Security Disability Insurance (SSDI) and the Supplemental Security Income (SSI) programs. The SSDI program is an insurance program that provides benefits to individuals who have paid into the system and meet certain minimum work requirements. In contrast, the SSI program is a means-tested program that does not have work or contribution requirements, but restricts benefits to those who meet asset and resource limitations.

The SSDI program was enacted in 1956 and provides benefits to insured disabled workers under the full retirement age (and to their

* This is an edited, reformatted and augmented version of a Congressional Research Service publication, CRS Report for Congress RL32279, prepared for Members and Committees of Congress, from www.crs.gov, dated June 11, 2013.

spouses, surviving disabled spouses, and children) in amounts related to the disabled worker's former earnings in covered employment. The SSI program, which went into effect in 1974, is a needs-based program that provides a flat cash benefit assuring a minimum cash income to aged, blind, and disabled individuals who have very limited income and assets.

To receive disability benefits under either program, individuals must meet strict medical requirements. For both SSDI and SSI disability benefits, "disability" is defined as the inability to engage in substantial gainful activity (SGA) by reason of a medically determinable physical or mental impairment expected to result in death or last at least 12 months. Generally, the worker must be unable to do any kind of work that exists in the national economy, taking into account age, education, and work experience.

Both programs are administered through the Social Security Administration (SSA) and therefore have similar application and disability determination processes. Although SSDI and SSI are federal programs, both federal and state offices are used to determine eligibility for disability benefits. SSA determines whether someone is disabled according to a five-step process, called the sequential evaluation process, where SSA is required to look at all of the pertinent facts of a particular case. Current work activity, severity of impairment, and vocational factors are assessed in that order. An applicant may be denied benefits at any step in the sequential process even if the applicant may meet a later criterion.

The SSDI program is primarily funded through Social Security payroll tax revenue, portions of which are credited to a Disability Insurance (DI) trust fund. In contrast, the SSI program is funded through appropriations from general revenues.

INTRODUCTION

Disability Insurance is generally intended to provide income support to workers in the event that an individual is unable to work due to illness or injury. Benefits may be provided by the federal government, state governments, or private insurers. This report presents information on two types of disability programs provided through the federal government: Social Security Disability Insurance (SSDI) and the Supplemental Security Income (SSI) programs. SSDI is an insurance program that provides benefits to individuals who have contributed to the system and meet certain minimum work requirements. In contrast, SSI is a means-tested program for individuals that meet certain asset and resource limitations; however, there are no contribution or minimum work requirements. Applicants for both programs must meet strict medical requirements to qualify for benefits.

SOCIAL SECURITY DISABILITY INSURANCE

The SSDI program is a part of the Old Age, Survivors, and Disability Insurance (OASDI) program administered by the Social Security Administration (SSA). The disability insurance portion of OASDI was enacted in 1956 and provides benefits to disabled workers under the age of 65 (and to their spouses, surviving disabled spouses, and children) in amounts related to the disabled worker's former earnings in covered employment. SSDI benefits, like those of the Old Age and Survivors Insurance (OASI), are meant to replace income from work that is lost by incurring one of the risks the social program insures against. Funding for the SSDI and OASI programs is primarily through a payroll tax levied on workers in jobs covered by Social Security, and the benefits are based on an individual's career earnings. In April 2013, more than 10.9 million disabled workers, spouses, and children were receiving SSDI benefits.[1]

SUPPLEMENTAL SECURITY INCOME

The SSI program, which went into effect in 1974, is a means-tested program that provides cash payments assuring a minimum income for aged, blind, or disabled individuals who have very limited income and assets.[2] This program is often referred to as a "program of last resort" since individuals who apply for benefits are also required to apply for all other benefits to which they may be entitled, such as Social Security retirement or disability benefits, pensions, or unemployment benefits. Although the SSI program is administered by SSA, it is funded through general revenues—not payroll taxes. The federal benefit provided through this program, unlike through the SSDI program, is a flat amount (adjusted for other income the individual may have), and it is not related to prior earnings. In addition to the federal SSI payment, many states provide supplements to certain groups or categories of people. At the end of April 2013, over 8.3 million individuals were receiving SSI payments.[3] Of these, more than 7.1 million were entitled to benefits on the basis of disability or blindness.[4]

TYPE OF BENEFITS AND AVERAGE BENEFIT LEVELS

SSDI

SSDI benefits are based on the worker's past average monthly earnings, indexed to reflect changes in national wage levels (up to five years of the worker's low earnings are excluded).[5] The benefits are adjusted annually for inflation, as measured by the Consumer Price Index for Urban Wage Earners and Clerical Workers (CPI-W).[6] Benefits are also provided to dependents (such as spouses or children), subject to certain maximum family benefit limits. Benefits may be offset if the disabled worker is simultaneously receiving workers' compensation or other public disability benefits. In addition, individuals who receive SSDI benefits also receive Medicare benefits after a 24-month waiting period.[7]

In April 2013, the average monthly SSDI benefit payment was $1,129.63 for over 8.8 million disabled workers, $302.61 for 160,710 spouses of disabled workers, and $336.95 for over 1.9 million children of disabled workers.[8]

SSI

The basic federal SSI benefit is the same for all beneficiaries. In 2013, the maximum SSI payment (also called the federal benefit rate), regardless of age, is $710 per month for an individual living independently or $1,066 per month for a couple living independently. Federal SSI benefits are increased each year to keep pace with inflation (as measured by the CPI-W).[9] The monthly SSI benefit may be reduced if an individual has other income or receives in-kind (non-cash) support or maintenance.[10] States may voluntarily supplement this payment to provide a higher benefit level than specified in federal law.[11]

SSI recipients living alone or in a household where all members receive SSI benefits are also automatically eligible for Supplemental Nutrition Assistance Program (SNAP, formerly food stamps) benefits and are generally eligible for Medicaid.[12]

Individuals may receive SSDI, SSI based on disability (or blindness or age), or both (some may also receive other benefits). The amount of the SSI benefit may be adjusted based on receipt of other income, such as SSDI benefits (the SSDI benefit is not reduced if the recipient also receives SSI benefits, because SSDI is not means-tested).

At the end of April 2013, the average monthly federally administered SSI payment was $527.95 for all recipients, $634.71 for children under the age of 18, $543.93 for adults aged 18-64, and $423.02 for adults aged 65 and older.[13]

ELIGIBILITY REQUIREMENTS

Definition of Disability

For both SSDI and SSI disability benefits, "disability" is defined as the inability to engage in substantial gainful activity (SGA) by reason of a medically determinable physical or mental impairment expected to result in death or last at least 12 months. Generally, the worker must be unable to do any kind of work that exists in the national economy, taking into account age, education, and work experience.

The definition of disability for disabled children receiving SSI benefits is slightly different from adults. Instead of demonstrating work limitations, children are required to demonstrate that they have "marked or severe functional limitation," and in addition, they are subject to slightly different criteria for the medical listings.

SSDI

To be eligible for SSDI benefits, a worker must be (1) insured and (2) disabled according to the SSA definition of disability. To be insured, a worker must have worked a minimum amount of time in employment covered by Social Security (similar to eligibility for OASI benefits). However, for disability benefits, if an individual does not have 40 quarters of coverage (generally about 10 years), he or she must have one quarter of coverage (one quarter of coverage is equal to $1,160 in 2013 and indexed to the annual increase in wages) for each year after 1950 or from age 21 up to the onset of disability. In addition, a recency of work test requires the worker to have 20 quarters of coverage in the 40 quarters preceding the onset of disability (generally five years of work in the last 10). Workers under the age of 31 need to have credit in one-half of the quarters during the period between when they attained the age of 21 and when they became disabled (a minimum of six quarters is required).

Once an individual's application for SSDI benefits has been approved, he or she will receive benefits after a five-month waiting period from the time the disability began, and will receive Medicare coverage 24 months after SSDI eligibility begins. Disability benefits will continue as long as the individual remains disabled, or until he or she reaches the full retirement age (FRA) when the benefits automatically convert to retired worker benefits.[14] SSA periodically conducts continuing disability reviews (CDRs) to determine whether an individual is still disabled. How often the beneficiary's medical condition is reviewed depends on how severe it is and the likelihood it will improve. The SSDI award notice explains when the first review is expected. If medical improvement is expected, the first review will be 6 months to 18 months after first receiving disability benefits. If medical improvement is possible, the case will be reviewed about every three years. If medical improvement is unlikely, the case will be reviewed only about once every five to seven years. If the beneficiary has received SSDI benefits for at least 24 months, a medical review will not be initiated solely on account of work activity.

As shown in *Table 1*, of the individuals whose SSDI benefits are terminated, the majority are due to factors other than medical recovery. In 2011, of the 653,877 disabled workers' benefits that were terminated, 51.7% were because of conversion to retirement benefits and 36.1% were due to the individual's death. Another 6.1% had earnings from work above the substantial gainful activity earnings limit, whereas 3.6% of those terminated had a medical improvement.

SSI

To receive SSI aged benefits, an individual must be at least 65 years old. To receive SSI disability benefits, an individual must meet the same definition of disability that applies under the SSDI program (see the section below on the "Disability Determination Process"). To qualify for SSI benefits because of blindness, an individual must have visual acuity of 20/200 or less with the use of a correcting lens in the person's better eye, or tunnel vision of 20 degrees or less.

In addition to age, disability, or blindness, an individual must meet income and resource tests to qualify for SSI benefits.

Table 1. Reasons for SSDI Worker Benefit Termination, 2011

Reason for Termination	Number of Workers	Percentage of Terminations
Total terminations/ suspensions	653,877[a]*	100.0%
Attainment of full retirement age	338,222	51.7%
Death of beneficiary	235,734	36.1%
Work above SGA	39,813	6.1%
Medical improvement	23,271	3.6%
Other	14,743	2.3%

Source: Extracted from Social Security Administration (SSA), Annual Statistical Report on the Social Security Disability Insurance Program, 2011, Table 50, available on the SSA website at http://www.socialsecurity.gov/policy docs/ statcomps/di_asr/.

[a] This excludes 2,078 (.3%) terminations for SSDI recipients that elected to receive an early, reduced retirement benefit, and 16 (.002%) terminations that occurred due to worker beneficiaries who did not comply with alcohol or drug abuse treatment programs or who refused vocational rehabilitation services.

An SSI recipient must also (1) be a citizen of the United States, or if not a citizen, (a) be a refugee, asylee, or victim of trafficking who has been in the country for less than nine years,[15] or (b) be a "qualified alien" who was receiving SSI as of August 22, 1996, or who was living in the United States on August 22, 1996, and subsequently became disabled; (2) be a resident of one of the 50 states, the District of Columbia or the Northern Mariana Islands, or a child of a person in the military stationed outside the United States;[16] (3) apply for all other benefits to which he or she may be entitled; and (4) if disabled, accept the vocational rehabilitation services that are offered.

The countable resource limit for SSI eligibility is $2,000 for individuals and $3,000 for couples. These amounts are not indexed for inflation and have remained at their current levels since 1989. Some resources are not counted in determining eligibility for SSI. Among the excluded resources are an individual's home; a car used for essential transportation (or, if not essential, up to $4,500 of its current value); property essential to income-producing activity; household goods and personal effects totaling $2,000 or less; burial funds of $1,500 or less; and life insurance policies with total face values of $1,500 or less.

Two types of income are considered for purposes of determining SSI eligibility and payment amounts: unearned and earned. Most income not derived from current work (including Social Security benefits, other government and private pensions, veterans' benefits, workers' compensation, and in-kind support and maintenance) is considered "unearned." In-kind support and maintenance includes food, clothing, or shelter that is given to an individual. Earned income includes wages, net earnings from self-employment, and earnings from services performed. If an individual (or a couple) meets all other SSI eligibility requirements, his or her monthly SSI payment equals the maximum SSI benefit minus countable income.

Not all income is counted for SSI purposes, and different exclusions apply to earned and unearned income. Monthly unearned income exclusions include a general income exclusion of $20 per month that applies to non needs-based income. Food stamps, housing and energy assistance, state and local needs-based assistance, in-kind support and maintenance from nonprofit organizations, student grants and scholarships used for educational expenses, and income used to fulfill a plan for achieving self-support (PASS) are also excluded from unearned income. Once the $20 exclusion (and any other applicable exclusion) is applied to unearned income, there is a dollar-for-dollar reduction in SSI benefits (each dollar of countable unearned income reduces the SSI benefit by one dollar).

Monthly earned income exclusions include any unused portion of the $20 general income exclusion, the first $65 of earnings, one-half of earnings over $65, impairment-related expenses for blind and disabled workers, and income used to fulfill a PASS. As a result of the one-half exclusion for earnings, once the $65 exclusion (and any other applicable exclusion) is applied to earned income, SSI benefits are reduced by $1 for every $2 of earned income. In 2013, the monthly earned income amount at which an individual with no unearned income and no special earned income exclusions no longer qualifies for a federal SSI payment (not including any state supplement) is $1,505 (also called the earned income "breakeven" amount); the monthly earned income amount at which a couple no longer qualifies is $2,217.[17] The earned income breakeven amount may be lower for SSI recipients with unearned income and those who do not live independently; it may be higher for those who receive special earned income exclusions related to a PASS or to work.

In some cases, the income and resources of non-recipients are counted in determining SSI eligibility and payment amounts. This process is called "deeming" and is applied in cases where an SSI-eligible child lives with an ineligible parent, an eligible individual lives with an ineligible spouse, or an eligible non-citizen has a sponsor.

In contrast to SSDI, the majority of adults who have their SSI disability benefits terminated are terminated because of having too much income. Unlike

SSDI benefits, SSI benefits may be suspended for one month, and paid in the next depending on an individual's income or resources.[18]

Disability Determination Process

The application process for SSDI and SSI disability benefits is very much the same. Although SSDI and SSI are federal programs, both federal and state offices are used to determine eligibility for benefits. An individual applies for benefits at a local SSA office where they are interviewed to obtain relevant medical and work history and to see that required forms are completed. The case may be denied at that point because the applicant does not have SSDI insured status or is earning too much money from work (work above the SGA earnings limit) in the case of Social Security disability cases, or is above the income and resource limits in the case of SSI disability cases— otherwise it is forwarded to the state disability determination service (DDS) for a medical determination.

The medical determination for both types of disability benefits is made on the basis of evidence gathered in the individual's case file. Ordinarily there is no personal interview with the applicant on the part of the state personnel who decide the claim.

The DDS determines whether someone is disabled according to a five-step process, called the sequential evaluation process. Current work activity, severity of impairment, and vocational factors are assessed in that order. An applicant may be denied benefits at any step in the sequential process even if the applicant may meet a later criterion. For example, a worker that meets the medical listings for disability but earns an amount exceeding the SGA earnings limit would be denied benefits at Step 1. The five steps are as follows:

- Step 1. *Work test.* Is the individual working and earning over SGA ($1,040 per month for a non-blind individual or $1,740 per month for a blind individual in 2013)?[19] If yes, the application is denied. If no, the application moves to Step 2.
- Step 2. *Severity test.* Is the applicant's condition severe enough to limit basic life activities for at least one year? If yes, the application moves to Step 3. If not, the application is denied.[20]

- Step 3. *Medical listings test*. Does the condition meet SSA's medical listings, or is the condition equal in severity to one found on the medical listings?[21] If yes, the application is accepted and benefits are awarded. If not, the application moves to Step 4.
- Step 4. *Previous work test*. Can the applicant do the work he or she had done in the past? If yes, the application is denied. If not, the application moves to Step 5.[22]
- Step 5. *Any work test*. Does the applicant's condition prevent him or her from performing any other work that exists in the national economy? If yes, the application is accepted and benefits are awarded. If not, the application is denied.

PROGRAM FINANCING INFORMATION

The SSDI program is primarily funded through the Social Security payroll tax, a portion of which is credited to a separate Disability Insurance (DI) trust fund.[23] By contrast, the SSI program is funded through appropriations from general revenues.

SSDI

The payroll tax is a 15.3% tax on earnings that is split equally between employees and employers. Payroll tax revenues are used to pay benefits under the Social Security OASDI program and the Medicare Hospital Insurance (HI) program. The Social Security portion of the payroll tax is 12.4% (6.2% each per employee and employer) on earnings up to the taxable maximum ($113,700 in 2013).[24] Of the 12.4%, 10.6% is paid to the OASI trust fund and 1.8% is paid to the DI trust fund. In addition to these payroll tax contributions, the DI trust fund receives some revenue from the taxation of Social Security benefit payments. These combined revenues are invested in non-marketable government bonds, which earned an effective annual interest rate of 4.1% in 2012.[25]

The resources in the DI trust fund are used to pay SSDI benefits and the costs of administering benefits. According to the projections of the Social Security Board of Trustees, the combined reserves of the OASI and DI trust funds will become depleted in 2033.[26] Individually, however, the Board of

Trustees estimates that the DI trust fund will become depleted in 2016, while the OASI trust fund will become depleted in 2035.[27] As higher rates of disability generally occur after the age of 50, the aging of the baby boom generation is a significant factor in the projected exhaustion of the DI trust fund. Addressing the growth in SSDI enrollment has been the subject of several reform proposals in recent years.[28]

SSI

The SSI program is financed through the general revenue of the United States. Appropriations for SSI benefits and program administration are considered mandatory spending. In FY2012, the net cost of the SSI program totaled $47.9 billion, including $44.2 billion in benefit payments.[29]

End Notes

[1] See Beneficiary Data-Benefits Paid by Type of Beneficiary, available on the SSA website at http://www.ssa.gov/ OACT/ProgData/icp.html. Select time series report by checking the relevant boxes for Disabled Workers & Dependents.

[2] See CRS Report 94-486, Supplemental Security Income (SSI), by Umar Moulta-Ali.

[3] Social Security Administration, SSI Monthly Statistics, April 2013, Table 1, available at http://www.ssa.gov/policy/ docs/statcomps/ssi_monthly/2013-04/table01.html.

[4] Ibid., Table 2 available online at http://www.ssa.gov/policy/docs/statcomps/ssi_monthly/2013-04/table02.html.

[5] The basic benefit formula for SSDI benefits is similar to the formula for retirement benefits in the OASI program. The worker's past annual covered earnings are indexed to reflect changes in national earnings levels. A formula that provides a higher replacement rate for low earners is then applied to these averaged earnings.

[6] A 1.7% cost-of-living adjustment (COLA) was applied for benefits in 2013. For additional information on the Social Security COLA, see CRS Report 94-803, Social Security: Cost-of-Living Adjustments, by Gary Sidor.

[7] See CRS Report RS22195, Social Security Disability Insurance (SSDI) and Medicare: The 24-Month Waiting Period for SSDI Beneficiaries Under Age 65, by Scott Szymendera.

[8] See Beneficiary Data-Benefits Paid by Type of Beneficiary, available on the SSA website at http://www.ssa.gov/ OACT/ProgData/icp.html. Select individual time series reports for Disabled worker, Spouse of disabled worker, and Child of disabled worker.

[9] See SSI Federal Payment Amounts for 2013, available on the SSA website at http://www.ssa.gov/oact/cola/SSI.html. A 1.7% COLA was applied for benefits in 2013.

[10] See CRS Report RS20294, Supplemental Security Income (SSI): Income/Resource Limits and Accounts Exempt from Benefit Determinations, by Umar Moulta-Ali.

[11] All but six states and the Commonwealth of the Northern Mariana Islands pay a supplement to people who receive SSI. Arkansas, Arizona, Mississippi, North Dakota, Tennessee, and

West Virginia do not pay a supplement. See Understanding Supplemental Security Income, available on the SSA website at http://www.socialsecurity.gov/ssi/textbenefits-ussi.htm.

[12] In California, SSI recipients are not eligible for SNAP benefits and instead receive a higher monthly SSI benefit. Specific Medicaid eligibility criteria are set by the states. For additional information, see CRS Report R41899, Medicaid Eligibility for Persons Age 65+ and Individuals with Disabilities: 2009 State Profiles, by Kirsten J. Colello and Scott R. Talaga.

[13] Social Security Administration, SSI Monthly Statistics, April 2013, Table 7, available at http://www.ssa.gov/policy/ docs/statcomps/ssi_monthly/2013-04/table07.html.

[14] For most of the Social Security program's history, the FRA was 65. As part of the Social Security Amendments of 1983 (P.L. 98-21), Congress raised the FRA from 65 to 67. The 1983 law established a gradual phase-in from 65 to 67 over a 22-year period (2000 to 2022). For more information, see the subsection entitled "Full Retirement Age" in CRS Report R42035, Social Security Primer, by Dawn Nuschler.

[15] Under Section 402(a)(2) of the Personal Responsibility and Work Opportunity Reconciliation Act of 1996, as amended [8 U.S.C. § 1612(a)(2)], the time limit for SSI eligibility for refugees, asylees, and victims of trafficking was nine years during FY2009 through FY2011. After FY2011, this time limit reverted back to seven years, the limit in place before the enactment in 2008 of the SSI Extension for Elderly and Disabled Refugees Act (P.L. 110-328). For additional information on the SSI eligibility of refugees, asylees and victims of trafficking, see CRS Report RL33809, Noncitizen Eligibility for Federal Public Assistance: Policy Overview and Trends, by Ruth Ellen Wasem.

[16] SSI benefits are not available to residents of Puerto Rico, Guam, or the United States Virgin Islands. Residents of these jurisdictions are eligible to receive federal benefits from their commonwealth or territorial government under provisions of Titles I, X, XIV, and XVI of the Social Security Act. These benefits are administered by the Department of Health and Human Services.

[17] This income break-even point is calculated by multiplying the federal benefit rate for 2013 ($710 for an individual living independently and $1,066 for a couple living independently) by two and adding $85. See Section SI 00810.350 in the SSA Program Operations Manual System (POMS), available online at http://policy.ssa.gov/poms.nsf/lnx/ 0500810350.

[18] SSI benefits are terminated if benefits have been suspended for at least 12 consecutive months.

[19] The Social Security Act specifies a higher SGA amount for individuals who are statutorily blind for the SSDI program.

[20] For the SSI program, there is no "severity test" for blindness.

[21] The medical listings can be found in the Social Security Administration publication Disability Evaluation Under Social Security, available at http://www.ssa.gov/disability/ professionals/ bluebook. This publication is commonly referred to as the SSA Blue Book.

[22] Cases of children applying for SSI benefits are not subject to the work test but instead to a test of functional capacity.

[23] See CRS Report RL33028, Social Security: The Trust Fund, by Dawn Nuschler and Gary Sidor.

[24] Section 601 of P.L. 111-312, the Tax Relief, Unemployment Insurance Reauthorization, and Job Creation Act of 2010 reduced the OASDI payroll tax—applied to the portion of the tax paid by the worker—by two percentage points for wages and salaries paid in calendar year 2011 and self-employment in calendar year 2011. Transfers would be made from the General Fund of the Treasury to the trust funds and earnings would be credited to the records of workers. While the payroll tax reduction was extended through the first two

months of 2012, Congress subsequently extended the reduction through the end of 2012. For more information, see CRS Report R41648, Social Security: Temporary Payroll Tax Reduction, by Dawn Nuschler.

[25] Data taken from the Social Security Administration Office of the Chief Actuary and is available at http://www.ssa.gov/OACT/ProgData/effectiveRates.html.

[26] The Board of Trustees, Federal Old-Age and Survivors Insurance and Federal Disability Insurance Trust Funds, The 2013 Annual Report, Washington, DC, May 31, 2013, pp. 2-5, http://www.ssa.gov/oact/TR/2013/tr2013.pdf. Projections based on the Board of Trustees' 2013 intermediate assumptions.

[27] Ibid.

[28] For more information, see CRS Report R43054, Social Security Disability Insurance (SSDI) Reform: An Overview of Proposals to Reduce the Growth in SSDI Rolls, by Scott Szymendera and Umar Moulta-Ali.

[29] Social Security Administration, Performance and Accountability Report for Fiscal Year 2012, p. 111, at http://www.socialsecurity.gov/finance.

In: Social Security Disability Insurance
Editor: Harvey Daniels
ISBN: 978-1-62948-776-2

Chapter 3

POLICY OPTIONS FOR THE SOCIAL SECURITY DISABILITY INSURANCE PROGRAM*

Jonathan Schwabish

NOTE

Unless otherwise indicated, the years referred to in this report are federal fiscal years (which run from October 1 to September 30).

SUMMARY

The Social Security Disability Insurance (DI) program pays cash benefits to nonelderly adults (those younger than age 66) who are judged to be unable to perform "substantial" work because of a disability but who have worked in the past; the program also pays benefits to some of those adults' dependents. In 2011, the DI program provided benefits to 8.3 million disabled workers, nearly sixfold the 1.4 million disabled workers who received benefits in 1970. Including the dependent spouses and children of those workers further increases the number of people receiving support in 2011 to 10.3 million. The growth in the program can

---

* This is an edited, reformatted and augmented version of a Congressional Budget Office publication, dated July 2012.

be attributed to changes in multiple factors, including demographics, the labor force, federal policy, opportunities for work, and compensation (earnings and benefits) during employment.

Over the past 40 years, outlays for benefits from the DI program (adjusted for inflation) have grown by more than nine times. During that period, the average benefit received by disabled workers rose from about $560 per month to about $1,050 per month in 2010 dollars. (Other programs also support workers with disabilities; for example, DI beneficiaries receive Medicare benefits that cost the federal government on average more than 80 percent as much as their DI benefits.) By comparison with outlays, revenues dedicated to the program have increased nearly fivefold since 1970. The divergence between the program's spending and revenues has prompted concerns about its financial sustainability. In 2011, spending on benefits in the DI program was $128 billion, or 0.86 percent of gross domestic product (GDP); by contrast, the program's revenues totaled about $94 billion, or 0.63 percent of GDP. In 2022, the program's spending and revenues will be roughly the same shares of economic output as in 2011, according to the Congressional Budget Office's (CBO's) estimates. By 2037, revenues as a percentage of GDP will be little changed, but spending as a share of output will have fallen slightly, as the proportion of the working-age population that is age 50 or older (and thus more likely to receive DI benefits) declines.

In this study, CBO in conjunction with the staff of the Joint Committee on Taxation (JCT) has estimated the budgetary effects of a variety of potential modifications to the DI program. In CBO's and JCT's estimation, two policy options that would alter the taxes that support the program would result in higher revenues of $13 billion or $28 billion in 2022. Seven policy options that would modify benefits could lead to declines in the rate of growth of the number of participants in the program and to cuts in the program's spending relative to CBO's currently published estimates; cuts in spending could range between about $1 billion and about $22 billion in 2022. In addition, CBO estimated the longer-run effects of each option relative to the agency's current long-term estimates: By 2037, the two revenue options would increase DI tax receipts in that year by 8 percent or 22 percent, and the seven spending options would reduce DI outlays by between 2 percent and 14 percent.

Modifications to the DI program would necessarily affect several other federal programs, including, most significantly, the Social Security Old-Age and Survivors Insurance (OASI) program, Medicare, the Supplemental Security Income (SSI) program, and Medicaid. However, analysis of those interactions was outside the scope of this report.

Restoring the DI program to a sound budgetary position would require combinations of the policies examined here or other changes to the program. From the perspective of the overall federal budget, the increases in taxes and reductions in spending considered in this analysis would improve the fiscal outlook to varying degrees but would leave very large imbalances between total federal revenues and spending if current policies were continued in all other respects.[1]

Alternatively, lawmakers could choose to modify the DI program in ways that would provide greater support to certain DI beneficiaries and increase spending for the program. CBO examined two policy options of that sort. Those options would increase DI outlays by $8 billion or $16 billion in 2022 and by 5 percent or 6 percent by 2037.

Policymakers could also alter the program in more fundamental ways. CBO reviewed proposals for several such changes, and this report summarizes the main themes among them. Modifications might include promoting disabled beneficiaries' return to work—for example, by moving to a partial disability system that related benefits to the degree of disability or, in the case of newly disabled workers, by focusing on rehabilitation and reemployment rather than the receipt of benefits. Many of those alternatives have been implemented in various European nations, in part to reduce spending on disability programs, and that experience may provide some insight into the options' potential effects. But the changes in policy that those countries have instituted generally have been in place for such a short time that their fiscal impact is uncertain. Overall, CBO concludes, such fundamental changes might help move the United States' DI program toward budgetary balance in the long run but are unlikely to provide sufficient immediate cost savings to resolve the program's near-term financial pressures.

What Is Disability Insurance?

The Social Security Disability Insurance program is one component of the framework of support that is the federal Social Security system, which comprises the Old-Age, Survivors, and Disability Insurance programs. The DI program provides income to nonelderly adults who have worked in the past but whom the Social Security Administration (SSA) now deems unable to work because of a medical condition that is expected to last more than one year or to result in death. Only workers who are younger than the full retirement age—established for the Old-Age component of Social Security—can be eligible for DI benefits.[2] Disabled beneficiaries receive monthly payments based on their past earnings for as long as they remain in the program.[3] (Some family members of disabled beneficiaries, including certain spouses and children, are also eligible for benefits.) If DI beneficiaries remain disabled and live to their full retirement age, they transfer to the Social Security retirement program at that age, but their benefits do not change.[4]

In May 2012, the DI program provided benefits to 10.8 million people. More than 80 percent of them, or 8.7 million people, were disabled workers; about 18 percent, or 1.9 million, were children of those workers; and fewer than 2 percent, or 166,000, were spouses of those workers.

The DI program's rules generally restrict beneficiaries from working and earning substantial amounts while they are receiving benefits. However, when beneficiaries first start to work, they can earn an unlimited amount for 12 months without losing their benefits. Thereafter, they can earn no more than some specified amount per year ($12,120 in 2012) before their benefits are eliminated. (A beneficiary may enter a "trial work period" during which he or she may work for nine months and remain in the program. A three-month grace period follows the trial work period.)[5]

The average monthly benefit for a disabled worker in May 2012 was $1,111; thus, at that benefit level, the average DI beneficiary this year may have an annual income of no more than $25,452 from those two sources. (For purposes of comparison, average income per person for the nation as a whole, according to the Census Bureau, was about $26,500 in 2010.) In 2006, the most recent year for which data are available, 50 percent of DI beneficiaries had household income that was below the federal poverty threshold—a proportion about five times higher than the national poverty rate of 10 percent at that time.[6]

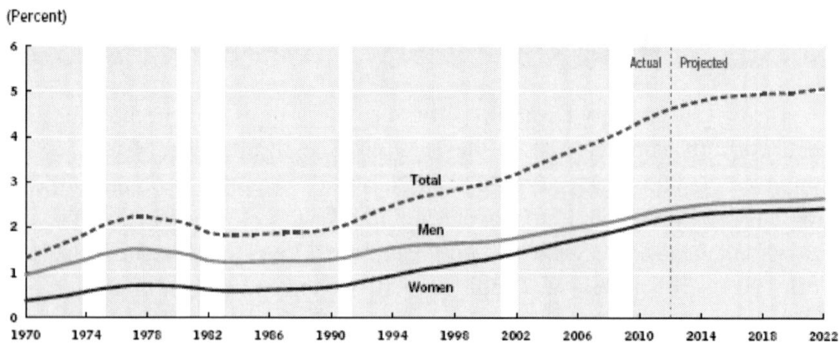

Sources: Congressional Budget Office; Social Security Administration.
Note: White bars indicate recessions.

Figure 1. Fraction of the Working-Age Population (People Ages 20 to 64) Receiving Disability Insurance Benefits.

HOW HAVE PARTICIPATION IN AND COSTS FOR THE DISABILITY INSURANCE PROGRAM GROWN?

Over the past 40 years, the number of disabled workers who receive benefits from the DI program has increased nearly sixfold, rising from 1.4 million in 1970 to 8.3 million in 2011. (Dependents of disabled beneficiaries are not included in that calculation.) In calendar year 1970, about 1.3 percent of working-age adults—individuals ages 20 to 64—were receiving DI worker benefits; in 2011, that fraction was 4.5 percent. Much of the recent growth in the share of the population that comprises disabled workers stems from increases in the number of women receiving disabled worker benefits. Between 1970 and 1995, the percentage of women who received such benefits grew by about 0.6 percentage points—about the same rate of growth as for men. Between 1995 and 2011, however, women receiving disabled worker benefits increased from 1.0 percent to 2.1 percent of all working-age adults; the corresponding change for men was from 1.6 percent to 2.4 percent.

Between calendar years 2012 and 2022, growth in the share of people ages 20 to 64 receiving DI benefits will slow considerably relative to growth during the past 40 years, the Congressional Budget Office projects. Nevertheless, in CBO's estimation, the share of people of those ages receiving benefits in 2022 will rise to more than 5.0 percent, with about equal relative increases in the proportion who are men and the proportion who are women (see Figure 1).

The rapid growth in the DI program's rolls has put increasing pressure on its finances. Between fiscal years 1970 and 2011, DI expenditures on benefits (adjusted for inflation) rose by more than nine times. As a result, a growing share of spending for the Social Security system is being directed to participants in the DI program. In 1970, DI spending was about 10 percent of OASDI expenditures; by 2011, that share had grown to nearly 18 percent. CBO estimates that by 2022, as the number of beneficiaries in the Social Security retirement program swells, the DI program's share of OASDI spending will shrink to about 15 percent.

Total DI expenditures were $128 billion in 2011 and, CBO projects, will be $204 billion in 2022. Measured relative to the size of the economy, DI spending was about 0.27 percent of the nation's gross domestic product in 1970; by 2011, that share had grown to 0.86 percent. CBO expects that proportion to continue to increase, to about 0.91 percent in 2013 and 2014, before declining slightly, to 0.83 percent in 2022. In contrast, revenues measured as a share of economic output were 0.63 percent of GDP in 2011 and, CBO projects, will be 0.65 percent of GDP in 2022.[7]

Total government spending on DI beneficiaries is substantially higher. In particular, the cost of Medicare benefits received by people who are eligible for them because they receive DI benefits was about $80 billion in 2011; CBO expects that it will be $120 billion in 2022. Moreover, some DI beneficiaries also receive benefits from the Medicaid and Supplemental Security Income programs.

The DI program's rapid expansion and the projected gap between its spending and dedicated revenues in the future raise questions about the financial sustainability of the program. Since 2009, the program has been paying out more in annual benefits than it receives in taxes and in interest on the balances in its trust fund.[8] CBO projects that the DI trust fund will be exhausted by 2016, nearly 20 years before the projected exhaustion of the trust fund for the Social Security retirement program.[9]

Why Has the Disability Insurance Program Grown So Rapidly?

Multiple factors help explain the DI program's rapid growth, and CBO has grouped them under three main categories:

- Changes in demographics and growth of the labor force,
- Changes in federal policy, and
- Changes in opportunities for employment and compensation.

Changes in Demographics and Growth of the Labor Force

Part of the growth in the DI program reflects the aging of the large baby-boom generation (people born between 1946 and 1964) and consequently the aging of the workforce, which has led to an increase in the share of workers who enter the DI program. Older workers are far more likely than younger workers to qualify for DI benefits. More older people suffer from debilitating conditions; moreover, the program's qualification standards for older workers are less strict than those for younger workers because older people are assumed to be less able to adapt to new types of work.

The aging of the baby-boom generation has shifted more people from the ranks of younger workers (ages 25 to 44), for whom the rate of enrollment in the DI program is lower, and into the ranks of older workers (ages 45 to 65), for whom the rate of enrollment is higher. Between calendar years 1996 and 2009—the approximate period during which the baby-boom generation entered their 50s—the share of disabled worker benefits awarded to older workers (age 45 and older) rose from 67 percent to 76 percent; mirroring that increase was the decline in the share of benefits awarded to younger workers (ages 25 to 44), which fell from 31 percent to 22 percent.[10] Thus, the baby boomers' aging would have boosted enrollment in the DI program even if no other factors had changed.[11]

Another reason for the DI program's growth is the increase in the labor force relative to the number of working-age people. That increase largely stems from a rise in the number of working women, who are eligible, like men, to receive benefits if they become disabled. The increased number of working women has boosted revenues for the DI program, through the payroll taxes collected on their earnings, but it has also led to more disabled beneficiaries and higher outlays for the program.

Changes in Federal Policy

In 1984, lawmakers enacted the Disability Benefits Reform Act, which expanded the ways in which people could qualify for the DI program. That legislation, in addition to reversing several of the cost-containment measures enacted as part of the 1980 Social Security Disability Amendments, shifted the criteria for DI eligibility from a list of specific impairments to a more general consideration of a person's medical condition and ability to work. The legislation allowed applicants to qualify for benefits on the basis of the combined effect of multiple medical conditions, each of which taken alone might not have met the criteria. It also allowed symptoms of mental illness and pain to be considered in assessing whether a person qualified for admission to the DI program, even in the absence of a clear-cut medical diagnosis.[12] The easing of the eligibility criteria increased the importance of subjective evaluations in determining whether applicants qualified for benefits.

Those changes in policy led to a substantial expansion in the share of DI beneficiaries with mental or musculoskeletal disorders, many of whom enter the program at younger ages than do people with other types of disabilities and many of whose applications are largely judged by using subjective criteria.

The share of beneficiaries with musculoskeletal disorders increased from about 17 percent in calendar year 1986 (two years after the passage of the law) to over 28 percent in 2010. The share of beneficiaries with mental disorders increased from about 22 percent in 1986 to about 33 percent in 2010. In addition to increasing the number of people who enter the DI program, those changes have helped boost the average length of time that disabled workers receive DI benefits because those disorders are comparatively more prevalent at younger ages and comparatively less likely than many other qualifying conditions to result in premature death.[13]

Another way in which federal policy has led to growth in the DI program is through the rise in the full retirement age for Social Security that has occurred during the past decade. That rise has had two main effects on the DI program: It has enlarged the potential pool of DI applicants by including more older workers who have not yet reached their full retirement age, and it has increased the length of time individuals spend receiving DI benefits because disabled worker beneficiaries now shift to the Social Security retirement program later than in previous years. (In addition, the rise in the full retirement age has boosted revenues for the DI program in the form of payroll taxes collected on the earnings of people who are now working longer before claiming retirement benefits.) Between 2002 and 2009, the age at which DI beneficiaries transferred to the retirement program rose from 65 to 66; it is scheduled to rise to age 67 by 2027.

Changes in Opportunities for Employment and Compensation

Whether people apply for DI benefits is strongly affected by the design of the program, the opportunities people have for employment, and the difference between the DI benefits an individual would receive and the compensation (earnings and benefits, including health insurance) associated with working. When jobs are plentiful, some people who could qualify for the DI program may choose instead to work. Conversely, when jobs are scarce, such as in economic downturns, some people with disabilities may find that their employment opportunities are especially limited, and they will instead choose to apply for DI benefits. Indeed, in the aftermath of the recent severe recession, applications for DI benefits reached a historic high, exceeding 2.9 million in calendar year 2010.[14]

Short-term economic downturns can have long-term effects on the DI program's benefit rolls. Many people who have been out of work for long periods find it hard to reenter the labor force, especially at their previous wage level, and they may ultimately turn to the DI program for support. Once they have been awarded benefits, only a very small percentage of DI participants permanently leave the program to return to the workforce.[15] CBO projects that as a result of the most recent recession and slow recovery, the number of disabled worker beneficiaries will continue to rise over the next few years (although growth will slow as the economy improves). That increase in participation stemming from the severe economic downturn will add to the long-term trend of rising enrollment.

The value of the benefits that a worker receives from the DI program relative to the earnings and benefits received through his or her job will also affect whether an eligible worker decides to apply for DI benefits. Workers who are displaced from jobs during economic downturns may face large cuts in their wages upon reemployment, making DI benefits relatively more desirable. Moreover, because the formula for calculating benefits is progressive, it replaces a larger share of earnings for low-wage workers than for high-wage workers. That progressivity combined with the growing gap between the earnings of low-paid and highly paid workers has probably increased the number of low-wage beneficiaries since the late 1970s.[16]

Access to health insurance and the cost of obtaining it are additional factors that can affect an individual's decision to apply for DI benefits. Disabled beneficiaries receive coverage under Medicare, regardless of their age, generally after a 24-month waiting period. For workers without employment-based health insurance, the eventual eligibility for Medicare that comes with participation in the DI program may be quite valuable and may encourage them to apply. Similarly, the recent decline in employer-provided health insurance might increase participation in the program not only by encouraging workers with disabilities to apply but also by discouraging those who are receiving benefits from leaving.[17]

The recently enacted Affordable Care Act is likely to influence future application rates for the DI program (especially after 2014, when new health insurance requirements are set to take effect under the law), but whether it will result in more or fewer beneficiaries is difficult to predict.[18] Among other changes, that legislation will make it easier for people who have health problems to buy their own insurance; it will also provide new subsidies for individually purchased coverage and expand eligibility for Medicaid in states that choose to do so. On the one hand, applications to the DI program may decline—because people who do not have employment-based health insurance will find it easier to obtain subsidized coverage as well as to gain access to health care without applying for DI benefits. On the other hand, applications to the DI program might increase—because some people who would lose employment-based health coverage if they left their jobs to apply for DI benefits will have access to insurance during the two-year waiting period for Medicare benefits, with no exclusions for preexisting conditions, through the health insurance exchanges that will be established under the law. Moreover, that insurance might be subsidized, depending on an individual's income.

APPROACHES TO ADDRESSING THE FISCAL IMBALANCE IN THE DISABILITY INSURANCE PROGRAM

Alleviating the financial pressures on the DI program will require a substantial increase in revenues for the program, a substantial decrease in the program's costs, or some combination of those two approaches. On the revenue side, options are straightforward but limited: To expand revenues, DI taxes paid by employers or employees (or both) must rise, or some other source of funding must be used. In contrast, options for reducing costs are both more complex and more numerous: For example, the components of the formula that is used to calculate DI benefits could be altered, as could one or more of the rules used to help determine eligibility for the program. CBO evaluated a variety of options that policymakers or researchers have identified, focusing on the following:

- The formula for computing benefits,
- The factors that increase benefits over time,
- Changes in eligibility that affect the number of workers who enter the DI program and the likelihood that people who are receiving benefits will leave the program and return to work, and
- Changes in the length of time people must wait to enter the program after they apply for benefits.

For each option, CBO assumed that the policy would take effect at the beginning of calendar year 2013. Estimates of the budgetary effects of the options during the next decade—which are derived from the agency's March 2012 baseline—are presented as nominal dollars in 2022 and as percentage changes from currently scheduled outlays or revenues; estimates of budgetary effects beyond the next decade—which are derived from the agency's June

2012 long-term budget projections—are presented solely as percentage changes in DI revenues or outlays from the projections for 2037 under current law (see Table 1).[19]

With a couple of exceptions, as noted below, CBO's estimates of the budgetary effects of the policies include savings or costs to the DI program itself and to the Social Security Old-Age and Survivors Insurance program when the effects on OASI are simply a result of DI beneficiaries' transferring to the OASI program.[20] (Benefits for DI beneficiaries who shift to the OASI program are paid from the OASI trust fund.) Modifications to the DI program would necessarily affect several other federal programs in addition to the Social Security Old-Age and Survivors Insurance program, including, most significantly, Medicare, Medicaid, and the Supplemental Security Income program. For the policy options presented in this study, CBO generally has not estimated the effects they might have on those other federal programs. (For a more complete discussion of such interactions, see Box 1.)

Table 1. Summary of Possible Approaches to Changing the Disability Insurance Program

	Number ofDisabled Worker Beneficiaries Affected in 2022 (Thousands)	Effect on DI Revenues or Outlays		
		Percentage Change from Currently Scheduled Revenues or Outlays		
		In Billions of Dollars in 2022	In 2022[a]	In 2037[b]
Increase Revenues		Reducing the DI Program's Fiscal Imbalance Effects on Revenues		
Raise the DI tax rate by 0.4 percentage points[c]	n.a.	28	18	22
Increase the amount of earnings that are taxable[c]	n.a.	13	8	8
		Effects on Outlays		
Change the DI Benefit Formula				
Reduce all benefits by 15 percent	6,200	-22	-11	-14
Reduce DI benefits for people age 53 and older	1,900	-6	-3	-7
Change How DI Benefits Grow Over Time—Reduce				

Table 1. (Continued)

Increase Revenues	Number ofDisabled Worker Beneficiaries Affected in 2022 (Thousands)	Effect on DI Revenues or Outlays		
		Percentage Change from Currently Scheduled Revenues or Outlays		
		In Billions of Dollars in 2022	In 2022[a]	In 2037[b]
		Reducing the DI Program's Fiscal Imbalance Effects on Revenues		
COLAs by Using a Different Measure of Inflation[d,e]	10,100	-3	-1	-2
Change Eligibility Rules				
Eliminate eligibility starting at age 62[f]	500	-12	-6	-6
Require applicants to have worked more in recent years	400	-8	-4	-5
Increase the age at which disability requirements become less restrictive	50	-1	-1	-3
Change Waiting Periods—Extend the Waiting				
Period for Benefits from 5 Months to 12 Months	900	-11	-6	-7
	Providing Greater Support to DI Beneficiaries—Effects on Outlays			
Increase the COLA by 1 Percentage Point[d]	10,100	16	8	6
Eliminate the 5-Month Waiting Period	900	8	4	5

Source: Congressional Budget Office.

Note: DI = disability insurance; n.a. = not applicable; COLA = cost-of-living adjustment.

[a] Changes are measured against CBO's March 2012 baseline; see Congressional Budget Office, Updated Budget Projections: Fiscal Years 2012 to 2022 (March 2012).

[b] Changes are measured against estimates in Congressional Budget Office, The 2012 Long-Term Budget Outlook (June 2012).

[c] Estimates of revenues for 2022 provided by the staff of the Joint Committee on Taxation.

[d] CBO's estimates for options affecting COLAs apply to all beneficiaries; estimates for all other options that change outlays apply only to new beneficiaries in 2013 and later.

[e] CBO's estimates for this option apply the reduction in the COLA to beneficiaries of the entire Social Security system—the Old-Age and Survivors (OASI) and Disability Insurance programs—and to recipients of Supplemental Security Income. The table shows only the savings to the DI program. Savings for all three programs would total $25.0 billion in 2022.

[f] CBO's estimates for this option apply the elimination of eligibility to DI beneficiaries only. The resulting savings are offset by an increase in OASI benefits of $9.3 billion in 2022, for a net reduction in Social Security spending of $2.4 billion in that year.

Box 1. Other Federal Programs That May Be Affected by Changes to the Disability Insurance Program

The Social Security Disability Insurance (DI) program is linked to many other federal programs, most notably the Old-Age and Survivors Insurance (OASI) program, the retirement component of the Social Security system; the Supplemental Security Income (SSI) program; and federal health care programs, including Medicare and Medicaid. Changes to the DI program that affected a person's eligibility for DI benefits could have an impact on spending for OASI, Medicare, SSI, and Medicaid. Changes to the DI program that affected the size of the DI benefit that a person received but did not alter the eligibility criteria for the program would generally affect spending for SSI and Medicaid but not spending for OASI or Medicare. Because of the additional time that would have been required, the Congressional Budget Office (CBO) has not estimated how the policy options considered in this study would affect spending for and participation in those other federal programs. (In a formal cost estimate for legislation, CBO would attempt to assess the combined effects for all of the affected programs.)

The Old-Age and Survivors Insurance Program

The reduced spending for the DI program that resulted from policy options to tighten its eligibility requirements would be partially offset by increased spending for OASI. The offset is partial because not everyone who would lose their eligibility for DI benefits would be eligible for OASI, and people who would be eligible for OASI would generally receive a smaller benefit under that program's rules.

Most people who became ineligible for the DI program because of a change in policy would probably apply for OASI benefits as soon as they became eligible for them, at age 62. The benefits they would receive from the retirement program would be smaller than those they would have received from the DI program, CBO expects, because retirement benefits are reduced for workers who claim them before the full retirement age (the age of eligibility for unreduced Social Security retirement benefits) and most people who lost their eligibility for DI benefits would claim retirement benefits at the earliest possible opportunity. (Individuals who claim retirement benefits at age 62 currently receive 75 percent of the benefit they would have received if they had been eligible for the DI program; that proportion is scheduled to decline to 70 percent by 2022.) In 2010, more than 7 percent of initial DI awards went to people age 62 or older; another 52 percent of awards went to people ages 50 to 61. (Changes in policy that are directed at older DI recipients, such as not allowing people age 62 or older to apply for DI benefits, would have a much greater impact on OASI than would policies directed at younger people because a larger share of the people affected would be eligible for OASI.)

Medicare

Because almost all DI beneficiaries are eligible for Medicare after a two-year waiting period, changes to the eligibility requirements for the DI program would also affect the number of people who were eligible for Medicare and, correspondingly, spending for that program. The effects would probably be significant: Medicare's spending per disabled beneficiary averaged about $10,500 in 2009, or more than 80 percent of the DI benefits that the average disabled beneficiary received in that year. Policies that reduced the number of people who were receiving DI benefits would also lower spending for Medicare. However, policies that decreased average DI benefits without reducing the number of people who received them would not affect Medicare's spending.

Supplemental Security Income

The Supplemental Security Income program was established in 1974 to provide cash assistance to individuals with low income and few assets who are also disabled or elderly. The disability standard is the same for the SSI and DI programs; however, the DI program provides benefits only to people with a sufficient history of work.

About 15 percent of DI beneficiaries concurrently receive benefits from the SSI program, and about 30 percent of DI beneficiaries received SSI benefits at some point during their first five years of eligibility for the DI program. Accordingly, policy options that increased or decreased spending for the DI program would tend to have partially offsetting budgetary effects in the SSI program.

For example, a policy option that lowered benefits from the DI program would increase SSI's costs, for two reasons: First, dually eligible beneficiaries would receive larger SSI benefits to partially offset the income from the DI program that they would lose, and, second, some DI recipients who were not currently eligible for SSI benefits would become eligible because their income would be lower as a result of the reduced DI benefits they would receive under the policy option. Thus, a policy that lengthened the DI program's waiting period for benefits would probably increase the number of people eligible for the SSI program and the average benefit that the program paid, because the policy would reduce beneficiaries' income to below the SSI eligibility threshold (or to further below the threshold) during the extended waiting period.

By comparison, options that increased DI benefits would generally lead to lower SSI costs. And proposals that changed the definition of disability in both programs would affect spending for both programs in the same direction.

Medicaid

The DI program is not tied specifically to Medicaid. But any policy that affected eligibility for SSI benefits would generally affect eligibility for Medicaid because in most states, SSI beneficiaries are automatically eligible for Medicaid. Thus, a person who is eligible for both the DI and SSI programs is usually eligible for Medicaid's coverage of his or her health care costs during the two-year waiting period for Medicare; those costs are shared by the federal government and the states. After individuals who are eligible for both DI and SSI benefits gain access to Medicare, Medicaid continues to cover costs and services that Medicare does not pay for.

A policy option that changed the number of DI beneficiaries or the program's benefits could affect federal Medicaid costs by shifting some people between Medicaid coverage groups that generate different federal payments to states, even if the option did not change the overall number of people eligible for Medicaid.

For example, beginning in 2014, the Affordable Care Act (ACA) will extend Medicaid coverage to additional low-income people in states that choose to undertake that expansion.[1] The federal government will pay a larger share of the costs for those new enrollees as compared with the federal share of costs for people who were eligible for Medicaid under prior law. As a result, the federal share of any additional Medicaid costs stemming from a change in the DI program will depend on whether an individual falls into the new ACA-coverage group or into a prior-law-coverage group.

Health Insurance Exchanges

Policies that changed the number of DI beneficiaries or the program's benefits could affect federal payments for premium or cost-sharing assistance provided through health insurance exchanges that will be established under the ACA. Beginning in 2014 under that legislation, certain people who do not qualify for Medicaid or for affordable insurance coverage from other sources will be eligible for subsidies to purchase health insurance through the exchanges. The amount of the subsidy for which a qualified individual is eligible will vary with his or her income. Policies that modified DI benefits would tend to alter the costs of those subsidies by changing the number of people who would be eligible for them and the amount of the subsidies those individuals would receive.

Revenues and Other Federal Programs

Changes to the DI program would have a smaller impact on revenues (apart from those dedicated to the DI program and those associated with the subsidies provided through health insurance exchanges) and on other government programs than they would have on the programs discussed above. Some of the policy options that CBO analyzed would affect tax receipts because workers and their dependents might work more or less and thus have more or less in taxable earnings. In addition, some of the policy options would affect benefits under the Supplemental Nutrition Assistance Program (formerly known as food stamps), which uses income and assets to determine eligibility. Moreover, the policy options would interact with workers' compensation programs.

[1] The ACA comprises the Patient Protection and Affordable Care Act (Public Law 111-148) and the health care provisions of the Health Care and Education Reconciliation Act of 2010 (P.L. 111-152).

In its analysis, CBO also evaluated two changes that could be made at the administrative level—in particular, how the Social Security Administration hires and trains employees who conduct disability application hearings and how the agency reexamines disability cases over time. However, because evidence on the effects of such changes is limited, CBO did not estimate their potential budgetary impact.

INCREASE THE PROGRAM'S REVENUES

The DI program is funded primarily through a portion of the Social Security payroll tax, which is split evenly between employers and employees.[21] (Self-employed workers pay the entire tax.) The total Social Security payroll tax is 12.4 percent and is applied to earnings up to a maximum amount that generally increases over time with average earnings nationwide. The DI program's share of that tax is 1.8 percentage points; in other words, the DI tax rate today is 1.8 percent, implying that employers and employees each pay a rate of 0.9 percent.

One approach to addressing the DI program's budgetary imbalance would be to raise the DI tax rate.[22] Based on analysis that CBO conducted with the staff of the Joint Committee on Taxation, restoring long-term balance (over the next 75 years) between the program's costs and revenues would require that the DI payroll tax rate be increased by 0.4 percentage points (or 0.2 percentage points each for the employee and employer), to 2.2 percent. At that rate, revenues would be higher than in CBO's baseline projection by $28 billion in 2022, JCT estimates. In 2037, revenues would be higher than CBO's long-term budget projection by 22 percent, in CBO's estimation. Such an increase in the tax rate would equalize costs and revenues, on average, over a 75-year time horizon but would leave a significant funding shortfall over the next few decades.

Another way to expand revenues would be to increase the maximum taxable earnings limit—that is, the highest amount of employees' wages subject to the DI tax. The earnings of workers in the highest income groups have grown faster than average earnings in recent decades. As a result, the share of all earnings covered by the Social Security program that were below the taxable maximum shrank from about 91 percent in 1983 to about 84 percent in 2010. By 2037, CBO projects, about 83 percent of all covered earnings will fall below the limit.[23] Increasing the taxable earnings limit only for the DI program (the limit for the other Social Security programs would not be raised) to cover 90 percent of earnings—that is, increasing the maximum taxable earnings limit for the DI portion of the payroll tax from its projected level of $113,400 in 2013 to $174,000—would produce an additional $13 billion in revenues in 2022 and increase revenues by 8 percent in 2037.[24]

Those two methods of altering the DI program's revenues would affect taxpayers in different ways. Increasing the rate of the DI payroll tax across the board for employers and employees would spread the costs among all people with labor earnings. In contrast, raising the maximum taxable earnings limit would increase taxes only for higher earners, leaving the majority of DI taxpayers unaffected. In terms of workers' incentives to try to work more hours or to work harder, policies that raised payroll taxes would have opposing effects: On the one hand, an increase in the tax rate for disability insurance would encourage affected workers to work fewer hours or to work less hard because they would keep less of each extra dollar they earned; on the other hand, those workers would earn less after-tax income by working their current number of hours at their current level of effort, which would encourage them to increase the number of hours they worked and their work effort. CBO concludes, as do most analysts, that the former effect outweighs the latter and that higher tax rates reduce the supply of labor.[25] However, the estimates presented here do not incorporate any changes in the supply of labor.

Reduce the Program's Spending

Options that reduce spending for the DI program would require scaling back either the number of beneficiaries the program serves or the amount of support each beneficiary receives. The challenge facing policymakers who are aiming to lower spending is to choose options that maximize savings while minimizing the harm inflicted on people whose disabilities prevent them from working.

Change the DI Benefit Formula

One way to reduce the costs of the DI program would be to alter the amount of insurance it provides by changing the formula used to calculate benefits. Like Social Security retirement benefits, DI benefits are based on a worker's past earnings and are calculated using a progressive formula that replaces more of the earnings of low-wage workers than of high-wage workers.[26] (That is, workers who have higher earnings receive larger benefits, but the replacement rate—the portion of a worker's earnings that the benefits replace— declines as earnings rise.) Specifically, the primary insurance amount (PIA) formula for DI benefits has three components, any of which could be altered by policy-makers (see Figure 2):

- Average indexed monthly earnings (AIME). The AIME is a measure of a worker's lifetime earnings. It is calculated as the sum of his or her earnings, indexed to compensate for inflation and for the real (inflation-adjusted) growth of wages in the economy as a whole, divided by the number of months over which the earnings were obtained.[27] For disabled worker beneficiaries, the AIME is computed by using an individual's indexed earnings between the age of 22 and the year of onset of his or her disability.
- Primary insurance amount factors. The PIA factors are the rates by which the components of the AIME are multiplied—specifically, 90 percent, 32 percent, and 15 percent. The PIA factors, which are fixed by law, have been at those levels since 1977.[28]
- Bend points. The dollar amounts of the AIME at which the PIA factors change are called "bend points." They govern the portions of the AIME associated with each PIA factor and change annually when the national average wage index rises. In 2011, the bend points were $749 and $4,517. Thus, a person with an AIME below $749 received a DI benefit equal to 90 percent of that amount; a person with an AIME between $749 and $4,517 received 90 percent of the first $749 and 32 percent of the remainder; and a person with an AIME above $4,517 received 90 percent of the first $749, 32 percent of the next $3,768 ($4,517 minus $749), and 15 percent of the amount above $4,517.

CBO analyzed two options that are based on modifying the formula for computing DI benefits.

Reduce All Benefits by 15 Percent. Policymakers could choose to reduce all DI benefits by the same amount, a change that would maintain the progressivity of the DI program. For example, benefits for newly eligible workers could be cut by 15 percent by reducing each PIA factor by that percentage (to 77 percent, 27 percent, and 13 percent). Under that version of the option, the average DI benefit for disabled workers in 2012 would decline from $1,111 per month to $944 per month. Outlays for DI would fall by $22 billion in 2022 and by 14 percent in 2037.[29]

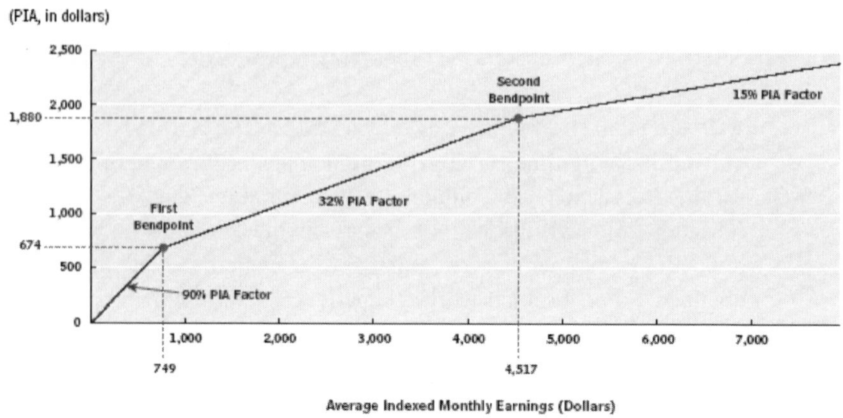

Source: Congressional Budget Office.

Notes: The section in the text titled "Change the DI Benefit Formula" on page 11 describes the computation of benefits. PIA = primary insurance amount.

Figure 2. Primary Insurance Amount Formula for Computing Disability Insurance Benefits in 2011.

Changes to benefits in the DI program would also directly affect other federal programs that use applicants' income and assets to determine eligibility or amounts of support. In particular, people whose DI benefits were reduced would be more likely to qualify for the Supplemental Security Income program and Medicaid. Lower DI benefits might also deter some people from participating in the DI program, which would reduce outlays in related programs, such as Medicare. However, if fewer people applied for DI benefits, outlays might rise in the retirement portion of Social Security if people then claimed their retirement benefits earlier than they otherwise would have. CBO did not estimate the effects of this option on outlays for programs other than DI.

Reduce DI Benefits for People Age 53 and Older. Under the current Social Security system, workers who claim retirement benefits at age 62 rather than at their full retirement age are subject to an actuarial reduction that lowers their benefits for as long as they live. In contrast, workers who at age 62 move from employment to the DI program's rolls, and then to Social Security's retirement program at their full retirement age, are not subject to a reduction.

Instead, they receive approximately the same retirement benefits in each year that they would have received if they had enrolled directly in the retirement program at their full retirement age. A potential change to benefits for DI beneficiaries would be to impose the same penalty on them at age 62 that is now paid by early retirees.

CBO analyzed the budgetary effects of such an option by considering an approach that would reduce newly awarded benefits for older workers on the basis of their age. Specifically, for people born in 1960 and later, CBO estimated the effect of permanently reducing an older person's DI benefits at the time the benefits are first awarded; starting at age 53, benefits would be reduced by 3 percent, with an additional 3 percent reduction occurring at each subsequent year of age. Thus, a person who was newly awarded benefits at age 54 (in 2014 or later) would face a permanent reduction in benefits of 6 percent, a person who was newly awarded benefits at age 55 (in 2015 or later) would face a permanent reduction in benefits of 9 percent, and so on. Ultimately, a new beneficiary who was 62 years old would receive a permanent benefit reduction of 30 percent, which is equal to the reduced Social Security retirement benefit at that age for workers born in 1960 and later. A new beneficiary between the ages of 62 and 67 (the full retirement age for that group of workers) would receive a benefit equal to the Social Security retirement benefit he or she would have received at that age.

If such a schedule of reductions was put in place at the beginning of 2013, the option would affect about 2 million people in 2022 and would reduce outlays by about $6 billion in that year and by nearly 7 percent in 2037, CBO estimates. Under the option, monthly support for people who were newly awarded benefits in 2022 would be reduced, on average, by between $50 (for 53-yearolds) and $600 (for 62-year-olds). Again, changes in the benefits provided through the DI program would directly affect spending for other parts of the Social Security system, Medicare, Medicaid, and SSI, but CBO did not estimate those effects.

Change How DI Benefits Grow Over Time

The DI program adjusts disabled workers' benefits annually to account for increases in the prices of goods and services. For those calculations, the program currently uses the consumer price index for urban wage earners and clerical workers (CPI-W); under this option, the program would switch to a different indexing factor—specifically, the chained CPI.[30] Over the next 10 years, CBO estimates, the chained CPI is likely to grow more slowly than the current CPI-W—on average, 0.25 percentage points per year more slowly. If that trend continued, this option would effectively reduce the growth of benefits for all DI beneficiaries. For example, the benefit of a disabled worker under current law might have grown during the next 10 years from $1,111 per month to $1,344 per month, but that same worker's benefit under this option (that is, indexation using the chained CPI) would grow more slowly, from $1,111 per month to $1,312 per month.

In CBO's estimation, DI outlays would fall by about $3 billion in 2022 if the chained CPI was used; in 2037, use of that alternative indexing measure would reduce outlays for the program by about 2 percent. If lawmakers decided to use the chained CPI simultaneously to index benefits in the Old-Age and Survivors' Insurance program, outlays for those components of Social Security would fall by over $20 billion in 2022. If they also applied the change in policy to SSI, its outlays would fall by nearly $2 billion in 2022. In contrast, if policymakers did not require use of the chained CPI for indexing SSI benefits, outlays for that program would increase slightly in response to the lower benefits that the option would provide to DI beneficiaries.

Change Eligibility Rules

The eligibility standards for receiving benefits from the DI program could be altered in numerous ways.

Eliminate Eligibility Starting at Age 62. As noted earlier, the DI benefits that workers receive at age 62 equal the full OASI (retirement) benefit they would have received at their full retirement age, a policy that encourages people to apply for DI and OASI benefits simultaneously. (Some individuals claim OASI benefits during the five-month waiting period that the DI program imposes on applicants for benefits. Those individuals' receipt of OASI benefits during the waiting period reduces their DI and subsequent OASI benefits for the rest of their lives.)

CBO estimated the budgetary impact of preventing workers from applying for DI benefits after their 62nd birthday or from receiving awards if the date they become eligible for benefits is after that birthday. Under such a policy, individuals who would have become eligible for DI benefits at age 62 or later would instead have to claim retirement benefits. Benefits for those men and women over their lifetime would be as much as 30 percent lower, on average, than the DI and OASI benefits they would have claimed. (The actual reduction in lifetime benefits would depend on their year of birth, the age at which they claimed retirement benefits, and how long they lived.) On the one hand, the option might induce some people to work longer than they would have worked under current law; on the other hand, it might induce some people who were planning to work until age 62 or 63 to leave the labor force at age 61 and apply for DI benefits. The option also would deny support to some older disabled people who would have relied on those larger benefits and on the associated Medicare coverage.

In CBO's estimation, the option would affect about 500,000 people in 2022 and would reduce DI outlays by about $12 billion in 2022 and by about 6 percent in 2037. However, most of those budgetary savings would be offset by larger outlays for Social Security retirement benefits as people shifted from the DI to the OASI program. OASI outlays under this option would rise by over $9 billion in 2022, CBO estimates, thereby reducing net savings for the Social Security system to about $2 billion.

Require Applicants to Have Worked More in Recent Years. To be eligible for benefits under the current DI program, disabled workers must generally have worked 5 out of the past 10 years.[31] CBO estimated the budgetary effects of a policy that would tighten that eligibility rule by requiring disabled workers to have worked 4 of the past 6 years. The tighter policy would reduce the number of workers who received DI benefits by 4 percent, CBO estimates, and would decrease outlays for the program by $8 billion in 2022. Expenditures on the program in 2037 would be about 5 percent lower.

Increase the Age at Which Disability Requirements Become Less Restrictive. One set of DI eligibility criteria for people who do not have a specific SSA-designated medical impairment is based on whether an individual can find a job within the U.S. economy. The criteria are known as vocational factors, and they vary with age, becoming less restrictive at ages 45, 50, 55, and 60 than they are at earlier ages.[32] For example, according to the current DI program's criteria, a worker who was 45 to 49 years old, whose "maximum sustained work capacity" was limited to sedentary work, who had no experience doing skilled work, and who was illiterate or unable to communicate in English would be considered disabled under the vocational criteria and awarded benefits if he or she had a sufficient work history.[33] In contrast, his or her younger counterparts would not immediately qualify for the DI program.

CBO estimated the budgetary impact of shifting upward the age ranges for the vocational factors. The current factors for ages 45 to 49, 50 to 54, and 55 to 59 would apply instead to ages 47 to 51, 52 to 56, and 57 to the full retirement age, respectively; the current vocational factor for age 60 and the factors for ages 45 to 46 would be eliminated. Under such a policy, the number of DI recipients would fall by about 50,000, or 0.5 percent, in 2022. Expenditures for the DI program would fall by $1 billion in that year, CBO estimates, and by 3 percent in 2037. By reducing participation in the DI program, the option would also reduce participation in Medicare (and thus Medicare outlays) but would result in greater outlays for SSI and Medicaid. CBO did not estimate the effects on outlays for those programs.

Extend the Waiting Period for Benefits from 5 Months to 12 Months

To be deemed eligible for the DI program and ultimately to be awarded benefits, applicants must have earnings that fall below a threshold amount—called the substantial gainful activity (SGA) amount—for at least five months, which constitutes a waiting period during which applicants receive no support from the program. For example, suppose a worker becomes disabled on January 15 and leaves the labor force. The worker then applies to the DI program for benefits, and SSA awards them to the worker on November 1 of that year. The worker's eligibility date is therefore July 1, or five months after the onset of disability, which SSA sets as February 1. (Unless the date of disability onset is the first day of the month, SSA pushes dates of onset to the first day of the next month.) In addition to receiving monthly DI benefits from November 1 onward, the worker also receives retroactive benefits for the period between the date of eligibility (July 1) and the awarding of benefits (November 1).

Increasing the DI program's waiting period would reduce outlays for benefits and might deter some people from applying. At the same time, if the waiting period was lengthened, it would make many disabled workers worse off because they would be forced to wait longer for benefits.

CBO estimated that under a policy in which the waiting period for DI benefits was extended to 12 months, DI outlays would fall by $11 billion in 2022 and by about 7 percent in 2037. Outlays for the SSI program, however, would be higher with that extended waiting period: People's income would be lower until they entered the DI program, and, in CBO's estimation, the increase in SSI spending that would result from that lower income would offset roughly one-eighth of the DI program's savings. CBO assumed that DI beneficiaries' eligibility for Medicare under this option would still begin 29 months after the onset of disability (the sum of the 5-month initial waiting period for benefits plus the 24-month waiting period for Medicare coverage once a disabled worker was awarded benefits), so spending for Medicare under the option would probably be little changed.

Change Certain Administrative Features of the DI Program

SSA could alter the administration of the DI program in a number of ways that might affect the program's costs. CBO identified two such potential changes: modifying certain aspects of the appeals process associated with applying to the program and altering how SSA reexamines disability cases over time. However, because there is little evidence as to the impact such policies would have, CBO did not estimate their potential budgetary effects.

Modify the Appeals Process for Disability Claims. The initial consideration and disposition of a disabled worker's application for benefits from the DI program are the job of the Disability Determination Services (DDS), which are agencies funded by SSA and administered by the states.[34] If a person's application is denied at the DDS level, the applicant can either terminate the application process or appeal the decision. Certain appeals may be adjudicated before administrative law judges— individuals appointed by SSA who conduct hearings at about 180 offices across the country.[35] Those officials are trained at the local hearing office at which they are employed.

Researchers have suggested different ways in which SSA could improve the administration of the DI program at the hearings level. They include modifying the selection criteria for administrative law judges, increasing the length of their training, and improving the consistency of training among localities.

Another example of a possible change in the program's administrative procedures involves altering the hearing process. Applicants for DI benefits are permitted legal representation at appeal hearings, whereas SSA is not. Policymakers could allow SSA to be so represented, which in the short term would add certain costs for hiring and training but might over the long run result in lower spending for the program because fewer people would be admitted.[36] However, the effects that any of those modifications would have on the disability determination process are uncertain, and CBO has not estimated their budgetary impact.

Increase the Frequency of Continuing Disability Reviews. An option related to recent growth in the DI program involves SSA's periodic reexamination of cases through continuing disability reviews (CDRs). CDRs help the agency determine whether disabled workers are still eligible for benefits, and they tend to lower outlays for the program because the average reduction in benefits associated with a CDR is significantly greater than the average cost of a review. The Budget Control Act of 2011 (Public Law 112-25) allows lawmakers to adjust the current limits on overall federal discretionary spending to permit additional appropriations for conducting CDRs. (That additional money may also be used to fund CDRs for SSI beneficiaries and redeterminations of whether SSI recipients still meet the program's nonmedical eligibility criteria—that is, those related to income and assets.)[37]

In its 2011 cost estimate for the Budget Control Act, CBO estimated the effect on outlays if the Congress appropriated the maximum amounts for which such adjustments to the spending limits could be made. In CBO's estimation, such appropriations would add about $4 billion in funding for SSA to CBO's baseline for the coming decade.

In addition, if that additional funding was appropriated, spending for benefits from the DI program, SSI, Medicare, and Medicaid would fall by nearly $12 billion during the 2012–2021 period, and additional savings would accrue after 2021.[38] CBO has not estimated the effects of even larger appropriations for such purposes or of other changes in the manner in which CDRs are conducted.

Options to Provide Greater Support to Disability Insurance Beneficiaries

In light of the importance of DI benefits to the individuals and families who receive them, policymakers might want to provide greater amounts of support to certain disabled workers. CBO estimated the additional federal spending that would result from two options for increasing such assistance:

- Increase benefits for all DI beneficiaries beyond their first year of receiving benefits by raising the annual cost-of-living adjustment (COLA) by 1 percentage point, and

- Eliminate the five-month waiting period for benefits for workers who apply for disability insurance, thereby paying benefits to DI recipients from the date of onset of their disability.

Increase the COLA by 1 Percentage Point

One way in which lawmakers could provide greater support to DI beneficiaries would be to increase the rate at which benefits grow over time. One consequence of such a change is that disabled workers who became entitled to benefits at relatively younger ages would experience more years of the enhanced COLA in their benefits than would workers who were awarded support when they were older.

If the COLA was increased by 1 percentage point, CBO estimates, total outlays would rise by $16 billion in 2022 and by 6 percent in 2037. Outlays for related programs would change slightly under such a policy: Spending for programs that used applicants' income and assets to determine eligibility for benefits (SSI and Medicaid, for example) would be affected because people who received higher DI benefits as a result of the larger COLA might not be eligible for those programs. CBO did not estimate the magnitude of those effects.

Eliminate the Five-Month Waiting Period

If lawmakers eliminated the DI program's waiting period for applicants, a worker would be eligible for DI benefits the day he or she was deemed to become disabled or to have stopped working because of the onset of disability. As under the current program, DI beneficiaries would receive a "retroactive" benefit—a lump-sum payment for the time between their application to the program and their approval for benefits.

Under a policy that eliminated the waiting period, total DI outlays would rise by $8 billion in 2022, CBO estimates, and by 5 percent of outlays in 2037. A policy that eliminated the DI program's waiting period would lead to additional DI benefits for disabled workers who would have been eligible for SSI and Medicaid, and it would therefore reduce outlays for those two programs. In particular, the reduction in SSI outlays would offset nearly one-tenth of the increase in DI spending.

POSSIBLE APPROACHES TO MAKING FUNDAMENTAL CHANGES IN THE DISABILITY INSURANCE PROGRAM

Changes in the U.S. economy, advances in medicine and technology, and the evolution of views about disability during the past several decades suggest that the DI program's model of disability, in which disabled people leave the labor force, may be outdated. In particular, those recent economic and perceptual shifts suggest that a disability insurance system that emphasized workers' continuing in their jobs might lead to a higher rate of employment among those with disabilities than is now the case.[39]

The effect of that kind of job-continuation model on the DI program's rolls and costs would depend on the structure of the changes in policy that established it, and only limited evidence is available on the potential impact of such changes. Therefore, CBO did not estimate the budgetary effects of specific changes of that sort. However, the agency reviewed proposals for such fundamental reforms to the DI program and summarized the main themes among them: moving to a so-called partial disability system or, for newly disabled workers, focusing on their rehabilitation and reemployment rather than on their receipt of benefits. In CBO's estimation, such changes are unlikely to provide significant short-term cost savings but could provide long-term savings or achieve other goals, such as improving the well-being of people with disabilities.

The Capacity for Work of People with Disabilities

At the time the DI program was established, in 1956, policymakers specified that beneficiaries be "unable to engage in any substantial gainful activity." Over the past half century, though, the labor market has changed considerably, shifting away from physically demanding jobs with rigid work schedules and toward jobs with a broader range of physical requirements and greater flexibility in how those jobs can be performed. That changed environment suggests there may be more opportunities today for disabled people to work. At the same time, views about people with disabilities have changed, emphasizing abilities rather than limitations, capacities over deficits. That modern view of disability was codified in 1990 with the passage of the Americans with Disabilities Act. The law requires that people with disabilities have equal access to employment (as well as to other activities) and that their employers make reasonable accommodations (for the use of such equipment as hearing aids and wheelchairs and through computer modifications to increase accessibility) to support their work.

Nonetheless, over the past 20 years, the employment rate among people with disabilities has declined sharply, from about 29 percent in calendar year 1990 to about 16 percent in 2010.[40] The drop in employment does not appear to be explained by a rising inability to work at all, nor does it seem to be attributable to the ups and downs of the business cycle. Instead, recent research shows that an increasing number of DI claims are coming from younger workers with mental or musculoskeletal disorders— despite other evidence indicating that those workers have the greatest capacity to remain part of the labor force.[41]

Another study, using data on accepted and rejected applicants with similar conditions, also found that some new DI beneficiaries were able to continue working.[42] To be sure, not all DI beneficiaries can be candidates for reemployment. Still, evidence of existing work capacity among disabled workers—as well as increased use of assistive technologies and workplace accommodations— implies that the design of the DI program might contribute to the relatively low rate of employment among people with disabilities.[43]

Encouraging Work Among DI Beneficiaries and Applicants

One approach that policymakers have already used to try to increase employment among current and future DI beneficiaries is to provide support for their return to work. As currently designed, however, that approach does not appear to have had a significant effect. In 1999, lawmakers authorized the Ticket to Work and Work Incentives Improvement Act, under which DI beneficiaries may request employment or vocational rehabilitation services. The act was designed to encourage DI beneficiaries to find jobs and lessen their reliance on the program's benefits. In particular, the legislation provided the following:

- Grants to support counselors for working beneficiaries,
- Upgrades to help SSA speed up the processing of information about earnings and the results from continuing disability reviews,
- Expedited reinstatement of disabled workers whose benefits were terminated because they returned to work but then became unable to work and returned to the DI rolls,

- Eased procedures for states to establish income and asset standards for working people with disabilities and thus share Medicaid costs through premiums or other cost-sharing arrangements, and
- Extended Medicare coverage—from about three years under the previous rules to nearly eight years under the 1999 legislation—for beneficiaries who returned to work.

Although those provisions reduce some of the potential hurdles to DI beneficiaries' participation in the labor market, the employment rates of DI recipients have not been measurably affected.[44] As of April 2012, 13.2 million DI and SSI beneficiaries were eligible for employment services through the Ticket to Work program, but only about 290,000 beneficiaries (or about 2 percent) were receiving them. About 1,000 firms have signed up to be "employment networks" to provide services to beneficiaries, and about 900 have successfully placed DI beneficiaries in jobs.[45]

The original Ticket to Work legislation asked SSA to implement and evaluate a demonstration project that would modify reductions in DI benefits for beneficiaries who work. SSA is currently evaluating the effects of such a program in which annual benefits are reduced by $1 for every $2 in earnings that exceed the SGA amount.[46] However, it is too early to determine whether those modifications will succeed in encouraging more DI beneficiaries to leave the program's rolls and return to the labor market.

A growing number of studies suggest that the critical obstacle to DI beneficiaries' return to the labor market is the substantial amount of time they have often spent away from employment, through a combination of looking for work, completing the DI program's waiting period, and receiving DI benefits. Specifically, because DI applicants must demonstrate that they are unable to undertake any substantial gainful employment, workers who seek support must generally leave any jobs they might be holding. Once an application is filed, the determination process is quite lengthy.[47] During the time a DI application is being reviewed, the applicant receives no income support or medical benefits from the program, and the law requires no additional accommodations for his or her disability in the workplace. Moreover, the program's limits on earnings discourage applicants from continuing to work even on a trial basis because doing so could jeopardize their DI application. Research has shown that returning to work is difficult for rejected DI applicants, and the time they spend out of the workforce (perhaps as much as two years while they seek benefits) generally makes it harder. For people who are eventually awarded DI benefits, concerns about maintaining that support and finding employment after a long absence from the workforce may keep many from reentering the labor market.[48]

STRATEGIES FOR REDUCING THE NUMBER OF PEOPLE WHO LEAVE THE WORKFORCE AND BECOME DI BENEFICIARIES

The limited success of programs designed to increase the rate at which DI beneficiaries and applicants return to work has spurred proposals aimed at supporting employment for people with disabilities before they quit their job to begin the application process. Ideally, such proposals can enable people with disabilities to remain in the workforce and can thereby slow the movement of such people onto the DI rolls. In the face of fiscal challenges that are similar to those confronting the United States, several other nations have implemented some of those types of changes.

Moving to a Partial Disability System

One way to encourage workers with disabilities to participate in the labor market is to move to a partial disability system of the kind used by the Department of Veterans Affairs and by many workers' compensation systems. Partial disability systems generally use a predetermined schedule to calculate a "percent disabled" rating for each individual; those percentages then determine the amount of the payments a person will receive. Such a system avoids the either/or threshold currently employed in the DI program in which employment and disability are considered incompatible. A partial disability system explicitly recognizes that workers with a disability that restricts their activity by, say, 30 percent or 50 percent have some remaining capacity to work.

If the DI program shifted to such a system, the number of people in the program would probably increase because the system would encourage people with less-severe disabilities to apply and qualify for benefits. Because current beneficiaries would not face reduced benefits and newly qualified individuals who are partially disabled would also receive benefits, outlays would rise in the short run. However, the net budgetary effects in the long run are difficult to estimate because they would depend critically on the definitions used to assess partial disability, on the amount of benefits provided for those who were so identified, and on the responses of workers and firms.

In practice, partial disability systems have been difficult to design and carry out consistently. Problems of implementation include, first, how to agree on a predetermined schedule of disabling conditions when the demands of a job and the severity of health impairments may change over time and, second, how to use the schedule to assess different individuals in a comparable way.[49] The difficulty of managing partial disability systems combined with rising costs—stemming from increased administrative expenditures and lost earnings among those with partial disabilities—has led several European nations (for example, the Netherlands, Norway, and Switzerland) to move away from partial disability insurance and toward approaches that directly involve employers in helping individuals with disabilities remain in the labor market.[50]

Involving Employers in Supporting Workers with Disabilities

Employers are not allowed to discriminate against people with disabilities and are required by law to make reasonable accommodations for them in the workplace. In most cases, employers have some financial incentive (such as the costs of replacement workers, retraining, and workers' compensation) to actively participate in keeping workers with disabilities on the job. However, because the DI program is funded through a flat-rate payroll tax on employers and employees, employers do not bear the costs associated with a disabled worker who stops working and becomes a beneficiary in the DI program.

In recent years, the policies of a number of European countries have changed to transfer more of the cost of providing disability benefits to employers. One way that has been done is by making employers responsible for paying benefits for a fixed amount of time. Those periods vary from as much as two years in the Netherlands to just six months in the United Kingdom, but like workers' compensation in the United States, the programs are meant to encourage employers to accommodate workers with disabilities and provide rehabilitation services in lieu of moving such workers to a system of long-term cash benefits.[51] Among the countries that have adopted the employer-involvement model, strategies are being developed to assist employers in managing their workers with disabilities.[52] One challenge with such an approach is determining the time horizon over which a firm is responsible for an ex-employee who enters the DI program.

Lawmakers in the United States could consider similar changes. Firms could be required to provide the first, say, two years of disability insurance, in which firms covered some portion of a worker's earnings before he or she was awarded DI benefits. Private-market provision of such short-term disability insurance—similar to arrangements in some European nations—might develop in that environment.[53] As an alternative to requiring firms to provide insurance, employers who did so, and whose private insurance agents cooperated with SSA in managing their cases, could be granted a reduction in DI tax rates. Firms that did not offer private insurance could be charged a higher DI tax rate, an approach that Switzerland has adopted.[54]

Another way in which European nations have encouraged employers to accommodate workers with disabilities rather than move them to cash benefit programs is by applying "experience rating" to the contributions employers make for disability benefits. In the context of the DI program, experience rating would mean raising the DI payroll taxes of firms whose workers became beneficiaries of the DI program at above-average rates or lowering the payroll taxes of firms whose workers claimed benefits at below-average rates. Experience rating provides a financial incentive for employers to engage in practices that promote continued work by people with disabilities.[55] The Netherlands and Finland use such a strategy, as do workers' compensation programs and the unemployment insurance program in the United States.[56]

One criticism of experience rating is that it could push employers away from hiring people with disabilities, potentially increasing growth in the number of beneficiaries in the DI program. That type of behavior is illegal and would come with significant costs if it was discovered. Uncovering and prosecuting such behavior, however, might be difficult.

End Notes

[1] For a discussion, see Congressional Budget Office, The 2012 Long-Term Budget Outlook (June 2012).

[2] The full retirement age is the age at which a person becomes eligible for unreduced Social Security retirement benefits. For details on DI eligibility, see Social Security Administration, Disability Evaluation Under Social Security (Blue Book), SSA Pub. 64-039 (September 2008), www.ssa.gov/disability/professionals/ bluebook/listing-impairments.htm.

[3] In this report, the term "disabled beneficiaries" refers to people with disabilities who are receiving benefits from the DI program as a result of their own disability and whose DI benefits are calculated on the basis of their own work history. (Such beneficiaries are also

referred to as disabled worker beneficiaries, disabled workers, or disabled insured beneficiaries.)

[4] For more-detailed descriptions of the DI program, see Congressional Budget Office, Social Security Disability Insurance: Participation Trends and Their Fiscal Implications (July 2010); and Social Security Administration, Disability Benefits, SSA Pub. 05-10029 (July 2011), www.ssa.gov/pubs/10029.html.

[5] Blind beneficiaries face higher thresholds; in 2012, they could earn up to $20,280 per year. For more information, see Social Security Administration, "Trial Work Period" (October 2011), www.ssa.gov/oact/COLA/twp.html.

[6]. Because the poverty rate among DI beneficiaries is measured at the household level and the national poverty rate is measured at the family level, the two are not strictly comparable. The household poverty rate among DI beneficiaries comes from Table 9 in Gina Livermore and others, Work Activity and Use of Employment Supports Under the Original Ticket to Work Regulations—2006 National Beneficiary Survey: Methodology and Descriptive Statistics (Mathematica Policy Research, Center for Studying Disability Policy, October 2009), www.mathematica-mpr.com/publications/ PDFs/disability/TTW_2006_NBS.pdf. The national poverty rate is calculated for all families by the Census Bureau; see Income, Poverty, and Health Insurance Coverage in the United States: 2006, Current Population Reports, P60-233 (August 2007), www.census.gov/prod/2007pubs/p60-233.pdf.

[7] Lawmakers have reduced the workers' portion of the payroll tax by 2 percentage points for calendar years 2011 and 2012; the reduction in tax revenues is being made up by reimbursements from the Treasury's general fund to the two Social Security trust funds. For the purposes of the calculations in this report, Social Security payroll tax revenues are considered to include those reimbursements.

[8] Federal trust funds, including those for Social Security, essentially constitute an accounting mechanism. In a given year, the sum of a fund's receipts along with the interest that is credited on previous balances, minus spending for benefits and administrative costs, equals a fund's surplus or deficit.

[9] Pursuant to the Balanced Budget and Emergency Deficit Control Act of 1985 (section 257(b)), CBO's baseline projections incorporate the assumption that DI benefits will be paid in full even after the trust fund is exhausted.

[10] Over that period, awards to people younger than age 25 rose from 2.0 percent to 2.5 percent. See T.A. Zayatz, Social Security Disability Insurance Program Worker Experience, Social Security Administration Actuarial Study 122 (Social Security Administration, May 2011), www.ssa.gov/OACT/NOTES/s2010s.html.

[11] See Mark G. Duggan and Scott A. Imberman, "Why Are the Disability Rolls Skyrocketing? The Contribution of Population Characteristics, Economic Conditions, and Program Generosity," in David M. Cutler and David A. Wise, eds., Health at Older Ages: The Causes and Consequences of Declining Disability Among the Elderly (University of Chicago Press, 2009), pp. 337–379, www.nber.org/chapters/c11119. Those authors estimate that the aging of the population accounts for about one-fifth of the growth in the share of the working-age population enrolled in the DI program.

[12] See Zayatz, Social Security Disability Insurance Program Worker Experience; Frank S. Bloch, "Medical Proof, Social Policy, and Social Security's Medically Centered Definition of Disability," Cornell Law Review, vol. 92 (2006–2007), p. 189; and David H. Autor and Mark G. Duggan, "The Growth in the Social Security Disability Rolls: A Fiscal Crisis Unfolding," Journal of Economic Perspectives, vol. 20, no. 3 (Summer 2006), pp. 71–96.

[13] Musculoskeletal disorders include, for example, certain disorders of the spine and major dysfunctions of the joints, which affect people's ability to ambulate or to perform fine and gross movements effectively. Mental disorders include, for example, certain types of affective, psychotic, and anxiety-related disorders. (Details are available at www.ssa.gov/disability/professionals/ bluebook/ AdultListings.htm.) Researchers have found that mortality rates vary substantially by diagnosis and that DI recipients with mental disorders and musculoskeletal conditions have lower mortality rates than the average DI recipient. See Kalman Rupp and Charles G. Scott, "Trends in the Characteristics of DI and SSI Disability Awardees and Duration of Program Participation," Social Security Bulletin, vol. 59, no. 1 (January 1996), pp. 3–21, www.ssa.gov/policy/docs/ssb/v59n1/index.html.

[14] In calendar year 2011, the number of DI applications dropped slightly, to just under 2.9 million; see Social Security Administration, "Selected Data from Social Security's Disability Program" (May 2012), www.ssa.gov/OACT/STATS/dibStat.html.

[15] See Su Liu and David C. Stapleton, "Longitudinal Statistics on Work Activity and Use of Employment Supports for New Social Security Disability Insurance Beneficiaries," Social Security Bulletin, vol. 71, no. 3 (August 2011), pp. 35–59, www.ssa.gov/policy/ docs/ssb/v71n3/index.html. Those authors found that over a 10-year period, about 4 percent of an entering cohort of new DI beneficiaries left the program to take a job.

[16] For additional discussion, see L. Scott Muller, "The Effects of Wage Indexing on Social Security Disability Benefits," Social Security Bulletin, vol. 68, no. 3 (December 2008), pp. 1–44, www.ssa.gov/policy/docs/ssb/v68n3/index.html; Autor and Duggan, "The Growth in the Social Security Disability Rolls: A Fiscal Crisis Unfolding"; and Kalman Rupp and David C. Stapleton, "Determinants of the Growth of the Social Security Administration's Disability Programs—An Overview," Social Security Bulletin, vol. 58, no. 4 (October 1995), pp. 43–70, www.ssa.gov/policy/docs/ssb/v58n4/index.html.

[17] Census Bureau, Income, Poverty, and Health Insurance Coverage in the United States: 2010, Current Population Reports, P60-239 (September 2011), Table C-1, www.census.gov/prod/2011pubs/ p60-239.pdf..

[18] The Affordable Care Act comprises the Patient Protection and Affordable Care Act (Public Law 111-148) and the health care provisions of the Health Care and Education Reconciliation Act of 2010 (P.L. 111-152).

[19] CBO's baseline is a neutral reference point for measuring the budgetary effects of proposed changes to federal revenues or spending. It consists of projections of outlays, revenues, and the deficit or surplus over 10 years calculated according to rules originally set forth in the Balanced Budget and Emergency Deficit Control Act of 1985. For more details about CBO's most recent 10-year current-law baseline projections, see Congressional Budget Office, Updated Budget Projections: Fiscal Years 2012 to 2022 (March 2012). For CBO's long-term budget estimates, see Congressional Budget Office, The 2012 Long-Term Budget Outlook (June 2012).

[20] CBO's estimate for the policy option that modifies the factors used to adjust DI benefits (that is, the option involving the chained consumer price index) includes the effects of applying that option to all OASDI beneficiaries and not just to those who shift from the disability to the retirement portion of Social Security. CBO's estimate for the policy option that eliminates DI eligibility starting at age 62 shows both the savings for the DI program and the costs to the OASI program for people who claim OASI benefits in lieu of DI benefits after age 62.

[21] In addition to payroll tax receipts, a portion of the income taxes paid on Social Security retirement benefits is credited to the DI trust fund. The government maintains a separate trust fund for the Old-Age and Survivors Insurance program.

[22] Another approach would be to redirect revenues to the DI trust fund from the OASI trust fund, a course that was followed in legislation enacted in 1994. However, such a redirection of resources would worsen the outlook for the OASI program.

[23] The maximum taxable earnings limit is $110,100 in 2012. Historical data are taken from Social Security Administration, Annual Statistical Supplement, 2011 (Office of Retirement and Disability Policy, February 2012), Table 4.B1.

[24] For those estimates, CBO did not assume that benefits would be increased to reflect the higher maximum taxable earnings limit. If benefits were increased to reflect that change, the net savings from this option would be smaller.

[25] For further discussion, see Congressional Budget Office, The 2012 Long-Term Budget Outlook, pp. 36–37.

[26] For a more detailed discussion of the Social Security benefit formula, see Congressional Budget Office, Social Security Policy Options (July 2010).

[27] Indexing ensures that a worker's benefits reflect the general rise in the standard of living that occurred during his or her working lifetime. Thus, a worker's nominal earnings for the appropriate working years are converted to near-current wage levels on the basis of changes in average annual earnings in the economy as a whole. For disabled workers, the calculations record earnings at their actual amounts for the two years before the initial computation of benefits and earlier earnings as indexed amounts. For a related discussion, see David H. Autor and Mark G. Duggan, "The Rise in the Disability Rolls and the Decline in Unemployment," Quarterly Journal of Economics, vol. 118, no. 1 (February 2003), pp. 157–205, http://economics.mit.edu/files/579. Those authors have shown that rising income inequality in the United States combined with indexing by the average wage level has significantly raised the earnings replacement rate for DI benefits provided to low-wage workers.

[28] For further discussion, see Social Security Administration, "Automatic Determinations: Social Security Benefit Amounts" (October 19, 2011), www.ssa.gov/oact/cola/Benefits.html; and Muller, "The Effects of Wage Indexing on Social Security Disability Benefits."

[29] In earlier work, CBO estimated the costs associated with the same option for the entire OASDI program and found that outlays for the Social Security system would decline by about 12 percent relative to outlays currently scheduled for 2040. See Congressional Budget Office, Social Security Policy Options, p. 21.

[30]. For a broader discussion of the effects of such a switch, see Congressional Budget Office, Using a Different Measure of Inflation for Indexing Federal Programs and the Tax Code (February 2010).

[31] For the purposes of computing Social Security benefits, a year of work is defined as having earnings that exceed Social Security's "quarters of coverage" threshold. In 2012, a worker receives one-quarter of coverage (up to a total of four quarters in the year) for each $1,130 of annual earnings. The amount of earnings required for a quarter of coverage generally increases annually at the same rate as the rise in the average wage index.

[32] Recent research shows the large increase in the rate of DI awards at those ages. See Joyce Manchester and Jae G. Song, "What Can We Learn from Analyzing Historical Data on Social Security Entitlements?," Social Security Bulletin, vol. 71, no. 4 (November 2011), pp. 1–13, www.ssa.gov/policy/docs/ssb/v71n4/index.html.

[33] See Social Security Administration, "Appendix 2 to Subpart P of Part 404—Medical-Vocational Guidelines," Code of Federal Regulations (November 2011), www.ssa.gov/OP_Home/cfr20/404/ 404-app-p02.htm. SSA's definition of "maximum sustained work capacity" is related to the kinds of tasks a person can perform at work, and its definition of "sedentary work" is related to the amount of weight a worker can lift or carry and the amount of time he or she can stand, walk, and sit. See Social Security Administration, "DI 25001.001 Medical-Vocational Quick Reference Guide," TN 6 (03-10) (May 2012), http://policy.ssa.gov/poms. nsf/lnx/0425001001.

[34] For details on the application and appeals process, see Congressional Budget Office, "DI: The Social Security Disability Insurance Program" (infographic, July 2012).

[35] Social Security Administration, Annual Statistical Supplement, 2011, Table 2.F1.

[36] See Autor and Duggan, "The Growth in the Social Security Disability Rolls: A Fiscal Crisis Unfolding"; and Social Security Advisory Board, Improving the Social Security Administration's Hearing Process (September 2006), www.ssab.gov/documents/ HearingProcess.pdf, and Charting the Future of Social Security's Disability Programs: The Need for Fundamental Change (January 2001), www.ssab.gov/Publications/Disability/ disabilitywhitepap.pdf.

[37] The law allows for similar adjustments to the spending limits for additional appropriations for Medicare, Medicaid, and the Children's Health Insurance Program to ensure that enrollees meet the programs' eligibility criteria, that claims are paid accurately, and that the programs are managed effectively and efficiently.

[38]. Congressional Budget Office, letter to the Honorable John Boehner and the Honorable Harry Reid about CBO's analysis of the impact on the deficit of the Budget Control Act of 2011, as posted on the Web site of the House Committee on Rules on August 1, 2011 (August 2011).

[39]. For further discussion, see Richard V. Burkhauser and Mary C. Daly, The Declining Work and Welfare of People with Disabilities: What Went Wrong and a Strategy for Change (AEI Press, 2011); and David H. Autor and Mark G. Duggan, Supporting Work: A Proposal for Modernizing the U.S. Disability Insurance System (Brookings Institution, Hamilton Project, December 2010), www.brookings.edu/papers/2010/12_disability_insurance_autor.aspx.

[40] See Employment and Disability Institute, "U.S. Disability Statistics: Current Population Survey" (various years), www.disabilitystatistics.org. For a discussion of the technical issues related to measuring employment rates among people with disabilities, see Burt S. Barnow, "The Employment Rate of People with Disabilities," Monthly Labor Review, vol. 131, no. 11 (November 2008), pp. 44–50, www.bls.gov/mlr/2008/11/ contents.htm.

[41] Till von Wachter, Jae Song, and Joyce Manchester, "Trends in Employment and Earnings of Allowed and Rejected Applicants to the Social Security Disability Insurance Program," American Economic Review, vol. 101, no. 7 (December 2011), pp. 3308–3329, www.aeaweb.org/articles.php?doi=10.1257/aer.101.7.3308.

[42] Nicole Maestas, Kathleen J. Mullen, and Alexander Strand, Does Disability Insurance Receipt Discourage Work? RAND Working Paper WR-853-2 (RAND, March 2011), www.rand.org/pubs/ working_papers/WR853-2.html. Also see Eric French and Jae Song, The Effect of Disability Insurance Receipt on Labor Supply, Federal Reserve Bank of Chicago Working Paper 2009-05 (revised July 1, 2011), www.chicagofed.org/webpages/ publications/ working_papers/2009/wp_05.cfm.

[43] See, for example, "Assistive Technology, Accommodations, and the Americans with Disability Act" (Cornell University, (December 2000), www.ilr.cornell.edu/extension/ files/download/ Assistive_Tech.pdf.

[44] About the Effectiveness of Fragmented and Overlapping Programs, GAO-12-677 (June 2012), www.gao.gov/assets/600/592074.pdf, and Social Security Disability: Ticket to Work Participation Has Increased, but Additional Oversight Needed, GAO 11-324 (May 2011), www.gao.gov/products/ GAO-11-324; and Craig Thornton and others, Evaluation of the Ticket to Work Program: Assessment of Post-Rollout Implementation and Early Impacts (Mathematica Policy Research and Cornell University, May 2007).

[45] For additional information on the Ticket to Work program and the employment networks, see Social Security Administration, "Ticket to Work," www.ssa.gov/disabilityresearch/ offsetnational.htm; and David Stapleton and others, Ticket to Work at the Crossroads: A Solid Foundation with an Uncertain Future (Mathematica Policy Research and Cornell University, September 2008).

[46] As under the DI program's usual rules, beneficiaries in the trial program are allowed to earn any amount for as long as 12 months (a trial work period of 9 months plus a grace period of 3 months) and keep all of their benefits. But also under those rules, beneficiaries lose 100 percent of their benefits after 12 months if they earn the SGA or more, whereas in the trial program, many beneficiaries can keep a substantial share of their benefits. See Social Security Administration, "Benefit Offset National Demonstration" (July 2012), www.ssa.gov/ disabilityresearch/offsetnational.htm.

[47] The average DI applicant who appeals an initially denied application to an administrative law judge will wait about 12 months for the case to be decided, although that is significantly faster than the time required for such judgments a few years ago. See Congressional Budget Office, "DI: The Social Security Disability Insurance Program" (infographic); Social Security Administration, The Social Security Administration's (SSA) Performance and Accountability Report (PAR) for Fiscal Year (FY) 2011 (February 2012), www.socialsecurity.gov/finance; and David Autor and others, Does Delay Cause Decay? The Effect of Administrative Decision Time on the Labor Force Participation and Earnings of Disability Applicants, University of Michigan Retirement Research Center Working Paper 2011-258 (September 2011), www.mrrc.isr.umich.edu/publications/papers/ pdf/wp258.pdf.

[48]. Maestas, Mullen, and Strand, Does Disability Insurance Receipt Discourage Work?

[49] The Institute of Medicine's Committee on Medical Evaluation of Veterans for Disability Compensation highlighted some of those challenges in a review of the Department of Veterans Affairs' disability system. See Michael McGeary and others, eds., A 21st Century System for Evaluating Veterans for Disability Benefits (National Academies Press, 2007), www.iom.edu/Reports/2007/A-21st-Century-System-for-Evaluating-Veterans-for-Disability Benefits.aspx.

[50] See Organisation for Economic Co-operation and Development, New Ways Of Addressing Partial Work Capacity: OECD Thematic Review on Sickness, Disability, and Work Issues Paper and Progress Report (OECD, April 2007), www.oecd.org/dataoecd/6/6/ 38509814.pdf.

[51] For a discussion of the differences between the programs of other countries, see Organisation for Economic Co-operation and Development, Sickness, Disability, and Work: Breaking the Barriers; A Synthesis of Findings Across OECD Countries, (OECD, November 2010), http://dx.doi.org/10.1787/9789264088856-en.

[52] See also the various OECD publications that make up the OECD series Sickness, Disability, and Work at www.oecd.org/els/disability.

[53] For details of such a proposal, see Autor and Duggan, Supporting Work: A Proposal for Modernizing the U.S. Disability Insurance System.

[54] Ibid. For further discussion, see Burkhauser and Daly, The Declining Work and Welfare of People with Disabilities.

[55] Ibid.

[56] Organisation for Economic Co-operation and Development, Sickness, Disability, and Work: Breaking the Barriers.

In: Social Security Disability Insurance
Editor: Harvey Daniels
ISBN: 978-1-62948-776-2

Chapter 4

TESTIMONY OF DAVID C. STAPLETON, SENIOR FELLOW, MATHEMATICA POLICY RESEARCH. HEARING ON "SECURING THE FUTURE OF THE SOCIAL SECURITY DISABILITY INSURANCE PROGRAM"*

Thank you, Chairman Johnson, Ranking Member Becerra, and members of the subcommittee for this opportunity to testify on the future of the Social Security Disability Insurance (SSDI) program. In my work as a senior fellow at Mathematica Policy Research and as director of Mathematica's Center on Studying Disability Policy, I have conducted numerous evaluations of programs and services intended to support people with disabilities, substantial research on their employment and economic status, and various studies of the factors that impede or facilitate their financial independence. I have also written and spoken extensively about the efficiency and cost-effectiveness of our nation's disability support system. My testimony today is based on this experience. SSDI is a key component of our nation's disability support system. That system is failing working-age people with disabilities as well as the taxpayers who pay for it. I will explain why and consider the implications for Congress.

* This is an edited, reformatted and augmented version of a testimony, presented September 14, 2012 before the House Committee on Ways and Means, Subcommittee on Social Security.

BACKGROUND

Of the approximately 17.5 million working-age people in the United States who live with disabilities, nearly 70 percent receive benefits from public programs. Despite increases over many decades in program participation and spending—$357 billion in fiscal year 2008, representing some 12 percent of all federal outlays—the economic status of people with disabilities has eroded significantly. As a result, reforms will require major structural changes to the nation's disability support system. Although such changes can potentially benefit people with disabilities and taxpayers, a policy transition that is too quick and not based on solid evidence could do more harm than good.

My testimony is organized into three key areas:

- An overview of the evidence that the disability support system is failing
- A discussion of the potential for systemic reforms that would provide better opportunities for people with disabilities to live fulfilling lives *and* that would rein in growth in federal and state expenditures for their support
- Action Congress could take to jump start a process of successfully restructuring disability policies and programs

The Failing Disability Support System

As you know, both the Social Security Administration (SSA) and the Congressional Budget Office (CBO) project that without legislative action, the SSDI Trust Fund will be exhausted in 2016. This outcome is a symptom of the failing public support system for working-age people with disabilities. Other symptoms include the following: the low and declining economic status of people with disabilities; very high and rapidly growing federal expenditures to support the working-age population with disabilities; persistent problems with the disability determination process; the large surge in applications on the heels of the recession; and a smaller, delayed surge in awards (Goss 2012).

The low and declining economic status of people with disabilities is the most important symptom of a failing public support system for working-age people with disabilities. For more than two decades, the employment rate and household income of people with disabilities have been falling steadily. (Mann and Stapleton 2011, 2012). By one measure, their employment rate was just 21 percent of the rate for people without disabilities in 2010, down from 34 percent in 1981 (Mann and Stapleton 2011). The median household income of working-age people with disabilities was just half the size of that for people without disabilities, down from 63 percent in 1981. The recession has greatly accelerated the rate of decline in the economic status of people with disabilities. (Kaye 2010).

The poverty rate for people with disabilities is very high and continues to climb. Over 30 percent of those receiving SSDI live in poverty, according to the official definition of poverty. When those who receive Supplemental Security Income (SSI) are included, this figure rises to over 70 percent (Livermore et al. 2009).

One study estimated that 65 percent of working-age adults with household income below the federal poverty line for at least 36 of 48 consecutive months have a disability (She and Livermore 2009). We also know that people with disabilities who live in poverty are much more likely than their counterparts without disabilities to experience material hardship, such as going hungry (She and Livermore 2007).

Federal expenditures on the working-age population with disabilities are both very high and growing rapidly. We estimate that, through 62 public programs, federal outlays to support people with disabilities in fiscal year 2008 totaled 12 percent of all federal outlays in that year—$357 billion. (Livermore et al. 2011; Stapleton and Livermore 2011). That's up from 11.4 percent of all federal outlays six years earlier—the last time we estimated federal expenditures for this population. The total is about half the size of defense outlays in that year. States added another $71 billion in 2008 to finance federal-state programs, mostly for Medicaid.

The biggest programs serving people with disabilities, measured by expenditures, are SSDI, SSI, Medicare, Medicaid, and Veterans' Health and Disability Compensation. Social Security benefits accounted for 31 percent of federal expenditures on working-age people with disabilities in 2008. If you add in the Medicare expenditures for Social Security beneficiaries with disabilities, Social Security disability beneficiaries account for a little less than half of the total federal expenditures for this population. Of course, some Social Security disability beneficiaries also receive other public benefits—SSI, Medicaid, veterans' benefits, food and housing assistance, and miscellaneous others—but we do not have full accounting.

In the past three decades, the increase in the number of SSDI beneficiaries has far exceeded the substantial growth that can be explained by growth in the number of disability-insured workers and changes in their age-sex composition. It is useful to compare current statistics to those from 1980, when Congress and the Executive Branch were so concerned about high rates of participation in SSDI that they substantially tightened eligibility. In December 2010, the number of SSDI beneficiaries was 2.2 million larger than it would have been had the proportion of disability-insured workers receiving SSDI within each age-sex group been the same as in December 1980—a 28 percent increase (Stapleton and Wittenburg 2011; see also CBO 2008).

Persistent problems with the disability determination process, the large surge in applications following the recession, and the smaller, delayed surge in awards after the recent recession are also symptomatic of the failing disability support system (Goss 2012). I will explain why later.

Key Problems: The Inability to Work Criterion for Eligibility and Program Fragmentation

There are two fundamental problems with the current support system. The first is the use of longterm "inability to work because of a medically determinable condition" as the eligibility criterion for SSDI and SSI—programs that, for many, are the gateway to Medicare, Medicaid, and other benefits. This criterion fails to recognize that many people with severe, medically determinable impairments can, in fact, substantially support themselves through work. Four of my Mathematica colleagues illustrate this point. All have very good jobs and do not rely on SSDI, SSI, Medicare, or Medicaid. Yet they have permanent medical conditions that meet the eligibility criteria in SSA's Listing of Impairments. One has a severe vision impairment, and one is deaf. Each of the other two is unable to walk and has other functional limitations because of physical conditions. If they stopped working for five months and told SSA that they could no longer work because of their disability, they would all qualify for SSDI. They are able to work despite their impairments because they have been able to achieve high levels of education they have received excellent health care, they can use technology and accommodations to greatly mitigate their functional limitations, and they have developed strong personal support networks. SSA would not consider these factors in determining their ability to work. My colleagues' impairments might have prevented people from working in 1956, when SSDI was introduced, but they certainly do not do so today.

My colleagues choose to work, rather than rely on benefits, because their careers are much more rewarding than a lifetime of dependence on public benefits, economically and personally. By making inability to work for medical reasons a criterion for support, the federal disability programs create a disincentive to work for those with significant medical conditions, foster long-term dependence, and increase poverty among the very people they are intended to help. Our support system essentially funnels people with severe impairments who do not have all of the advantages of my colleagues into a life of dependence on public support rather than helping them to become self-sufficient. Instead of helping people achieve their full potential, the current disability support system has created a poverty trap (Stapleton et al. 2007).

The inability to work criterion is a fundamental reason why the disability determination process is so problematic—it requires SSA to assess whether people can work on the basis of medically determinable conditions alone—literally an impossible task. It also explains the surge in applications and awards following the recession; workers like my colleagues with disabilities can use SSDI as an extended unemployment insurance program when they are laid off for other reasons.

The second fundamental flaw in the current support system, program fragmentation, has been amply documented by the Government Accountability Office (GAO 2005, 2008). A patchwork of federal and state disability support programs has created pervasive inefficiencies, including overlaps and gaps in services, misaligned incentives, and conflicting objectives.

Of relevance to SSDI, states have incentives to help young adults with severe impairments enter SSDI. Under current rules, people age 24 and younger can meet the work history requirement by earning as little as $4,520 per year for just one and a half years. On a monthly basis, that's less than 40 percent of the amount that SSA uses to define "work" for non-blind beneficiaries—the substantial gainful activity (SGA) amount. If an individual is enrolled in Medicaid or receiving other health benefits from state programs, that person's entry into SSDI will eventually result in the shifting of some state Medicaid expenditures to federal Medicare expenditures. State expenditures for some other services, such as mental health care, might also shift to Medicare upon a person's entry into SSDI.

State welfare agencies have a strong incentive to help their Temporary Assistance for Needy Family (TANF) beneficiaries enter SSI; under current rules, the agency gets to keep all of the TANF benefit savings. State vocational rehabilitation (VR) agencies also have an incentive to help clients who are not on SSDI or SSI to enter these programs. SSA might pay for the VR services if a client becomes a beneficiary, but it will not pay for the services if a client is not a beneficiary.

Social Security Policy Reform

Both logic and a growing body of evidence suggest that there are systemic reforms that would provide better economic opportunities for people with disabilities *and* reduce growth in federal and state expenditures for their support. I call them "win-win" policy reforms. Policy changes that put more emphasis on helping people with disabilities take advantage of their capabilities—especially before entering SSDI— and can potentially increase their income while reducing public support.

Similarly, program integration and/or coordination efforts that address the pervasive inefficiencies caused by program fragmentation could potentially improve outcomes for individuals while reducing the growth in expenditures.

That's fine in theory, but where is the evidence? The evidence is substantial, although in my view, it is not rich enough to move ahead with systemic reforms. A basic piece of evidence is that we've had better outcomes in the past without the important advantage of today's technologies and medical knowledge. The relative employment and household income of people with disabilities was much higher in 1980 than it is today, and SSDI participation was much lower (Stapleton and Wittenburg 2011).

Other evidence comes from several recent, methodologically strong studies. They have demonstrated that a small but significant share of SSDI beneficiaries would be working now if they were not eligible for SSDI (Chen and Van der Klaauw 2008; French and Song 2011; Maestas et al. forthcoming; Von Wachter et al. 2011). For instance, one study demonstrated that, in the absence of SSDI, 18 percent of new SSDI beneficiaries would earn above the SGA level (Maestas et al. forthcoming). Given the current number of SSDI entrants, this suggests that about 200,000 entrants each year can earn at a level that would make them ineligible for SSDI—perhaps not at the time they enter, but soon thereafter. With a work-oriented support system in place, that percentage might well be higher.

There is also a significant body of evidence that private disability insurers and workers' compensation insurers can and do help some workers successfully return to work after the onset of severe impairments (McLaren et al. 2010).

There is a smaller, but growing body of evidence that more work-oriented policies for youth and young adults with disabilities can lead to greater employment. The evidence is especially strong for those with psychiatric disorders (Burke-Miller et al. 2012), the primary impairment of over 15 percent of new entrants. More evidence is starting to emerge from SSA's Youth Transition Demonstration (Fraker and Rangarajan 2009).

Finally, there is a growing body of evidence in other countries with advanced economies that are experimenting with pro-work policy changes (Organization for Economic Cooperation and Development 2010; Burkhauser and Daly 2011). The Netherlands and the United Kingdom are the most obvious examples. Their work-oriented policy reforms are, of course, controversial, and the information about the impacts on the economic status of those affected is very limited, but it is quite clear that the reforms are reducing entry into public long-term disability benefit programs. It also must be said that our ability to learn from other countries' efforts is limited by institutional and cultural differences. But nonetheless, there are important lessons to learn from their reforms.

Roadblocks to Major Structural Reform

The evidence base is not strong enough to proceed with major structural reforms on a timetable that would address the exhaustion of the SSDI Trust Fund. The risks would be too high. If disability policies and programs were restructured on the basis of what we know now, there is a good chance that the reforms would not be win-win. As a group, people with disabilities might be worse off, or growth in public expenditures for their support might accelerate, or both.

For example, at least two proposals are designed to reduce the number of workers entering SSDI by increasing incentives for employers to retain workers after the onset of a disability (Autor and Duggan 2010; Burkhauser and Daly 2011. See also Social Security Advisory Board, 2006, MacDonald and O'Neil 2006, and Stapleton et al. 2009). There are, however, significant concerns about the consequences of these policies. First, they could lead employers to avoid hiring people perceived to be at high risk for SSDI entry. Second, people who are truly unable to work may find their path to SSDI strewn with even bigger hurdles than under current policy. Third, implementing these policies could reduce the competitiveness of U.S. employers in a global economy. I think these concerns can potentially be addressed through details of the policy design, but current evidence is not adequate for that purpose. Nor is it sufficient to support political consensus on such reforms.

What Can Congress Do?

Congress could put the country on a path toward successful restructuring of disability policy by taking steps that go beyond short-term fixes to the SSDI Trust Fund problem. (This section draws heavily on Mann and Stapleton 2011, 2012.) One might hope that existing programs would gradually evolve to successfully address work disincentives and fragmentation. That is not likely to happen, however, without a congressional initiative. Programs that will realize savings from increased employment and reduced reliance on public benefits—primarily SSDI, SSI, Medicare and Medicaid—are the responsibility of agencies other than those agencies best situated to implement work-oriented reforms—Education and Labor. This fragmentation is mirrored in Congress, where different committees have responsibilities for the different programs. Structural reforms require collaboration across committees—not unheard of, but not easy.

States also have to play a significant role in developing structural reforms because they administer and provide some of the financing for many disability supports. In the absence of congressional action, states might take the initiative on behalf of their disabled residents, but that rarely occurs, in part because states will realize only a fraction of any program savings and in part because they are hindered by having to obtain waivers from multiple federal programs.

The fragmentation in responsibilities for disability policies and programs helps explain why the United States lags behind many other countries in the restructuring of disability policy. Legislation is needed to jump start a process that would eventually lead to successful structural reforms. Potential legislation might do some of the following:

- Create a national disability policy reform commission
- Encourage the implementation and evaluation of pilot projects
- Define objectives and requirements for such projects
- Ensure that risks to subjects in pilot projects are minimized
- Foster a spirit of innovation and learning

- Allow considerable time to develop the evidence base that will support agreement on fundamental reforms

In the absence of progress toward win-win structural reforms, Congress will face increasingly difficult choices. To prevent the exhaustion of the SSDI Trust Fund, members of Congress have to come up with a politically acceptable combination of benefit cuts and increased revenues. I don't know of a public servant who relishes the idea of taking benefits away from people with disabilities. Americans have always displayed great willingness to provide support to people with disabilities. That's an important reason why federal outlays for their support constitute such a large share of all federal spending. But the alternative, increasing revenues, may be just as difficult.

As you continue to address the immediate Trust Fund problem, I would encourage your committee, in collaboration with other relevant congressional committees, to consider legislation that would initiate a process of long-lasting, fundamental reforms to American disability policies and programs.

References

Autor, David, and Mark Duggan. "Supported Work: A Proposal for Modernizing the U.S. Disability Insurance System." Washington, DC: Center for American Progress and Hamilton Project, 2010.

Burkhauser, Richard V., and Mary C. Daly. "The Declining Work and Welfare of People with Disabilities." Washington, DC: American Enterprise Institute, 2011.

Burke-Miller, J., L.A. Razzano, D.D. Grey, C.R. Blyler, and J.A. Cook. "Supported Employment Outcomes for Transition Age Youth and Young Adults." *Psychiatric Rehabilitation Journal*, vol. 35, no. 3, winter 2012, pp. 171–179.

Chen, S., and W. van der Klaauw. "The Work Disincentive Effects of the Disability Insurance Program in the 1990s." *Journal of Econometrics*, vol. 142, no. 2, 2008, pp. 757–784.

Congressional Budget Office. "Social Security Disability Insurance: Participation Trends and Their Fiscal Implications." Washington, DC: CBO, 2010.

Fraker, Thomas, and Anu Rangarajan. "The Social Security Administration's Youth Transition Demonstration Projects." *Journal of Vocational Rehabilitation*, vol. 30, no. 3, 2009, pp. 223–240.

French, Eric, and Jae Song. "The Effect of Disability Insurance Receipt on Labor Supply." WP 2009-05. Revised July 1, 2011. Chicago: Federal Reserve Bank of Chicago, 2011.

Goss, Steven. "Why Are More People Claiming Social Security Disability Benefits?" Presentation to the National Academy of Social Insurance Session in the House Cannon Office Building, Washington, DC, April 3, 2012.

Government Accountability Office. "Federal Disability Assistance: Wide Array of Programs Needs to Be Examined in Light of 21st Century Challenges." GAO-05-626. Washington, DC: Government Accountability Office, 2005.

Government Accountability Office. "Federal Disability Programs: More Strategic Coordination Could Help Overcome Challenges to Needed Transformation." GAO-08-635. Washington, DC: Government Accountability Office, 2008.

Kaye, H. Stephen. "The Impact of the 2007–2009 Recession on Workers with Disabilities." *Monthly Labor Review*, October 2010, pp. 19–30.

Livermore, Gina, David Stapleton, and Allison Roche. "Characteristics, Employment, and Sources of Support Among Working-Age SSI and DI Beneficiaries." Report no. 2. In Work Activity and Use of Employment Supports Under the Original Ticket to Work Regulations. Washington, DC: Mathematica Policy Research, 2009.

Livermore, Gina A., David C. Stapleton and Meghan O'Toole. "Health Care Costs Are a Key Driver of Growth in Federal and State Assistance to Working-Age People with Disabilities." *Health Affairs,* vol. 30, no. 9, 2011, pp. 1664–1672.

MacDonald, Bryon R., and Megan O'Neil. "Being American: The Way Out of Poverty: The Discussion to Transform Social Security, Medicare and Disability Tax Law. Strengthen What Works. Fix What's Broken." Oakland, CA: World Institute on Disability, 2006.

Maestas, Nicole, Kathleen Mullen, and Alexander Strand. "Does Disability Insurance Receipt Discourage Work? Using Examiner Assignment to Estimate Causal Effects of SSDI Receipt." *American Economic Review*, forthcoming.

Mann, David R., and David C. Stapleton. "Fiscal Austerity and the Transition to Twenty-First Century Disability Policy: A Road Map." Working paper. Washington, DC: Mathematica Policy Research, November 2011.

Mann, David R., and David C. Stapleton. "A Roadmap to a 21st Century Disability Policy." Disability Policy Issue Brief No. 12-01. Washington, DC: Center for Studying Disability Policy, January 2012.

McLaren, Christopher F., Robert T. Reville, and Seth A. Seabury. "How Effective Are Employer Return to Work Programs?" Working Paper WR-745-CHSWC. Santa Monica, CA: RAND, 2010.

Organization for Economic Co-operation and Development. *Sickness, Disability and Work.* Paris, France: Organization for Economic Co-operation and Development, 2010.

Social Security Advisory Board. "A Disability System for the 21st Century." Washington, DC: Social Security Advisory Board, 2006.

She, Peiyun, and Gina A. Livermore. "Long-Term Poverty and Disability Among Working-Age Adults." *Journal of Disability Policy Studies*, vol. 19, no. 4, 2009, pp. 244–256.

She, Peiyun, and Gina A. Livermore. "Material Hardship, Disability, and Poverty Among Working-Age Adults." *Social Science Quarterly*, vol. 88, no. 4, 2007, pp. 970–989.

Stapleton, David, and Gina Livermore. "Costs, Cuts, and Consequences: Charting a New Course for Working-Age People with Disabilities." Disability Policy Issue Brief No. 11-03. Washington, DC: Center for Studying Disability Policy, 2011.

Stapleton, David C., and David C. Wittenburg. "The SSDI Trust Fund: New Solutions to an Old Problem." Issue Brief Report No. 11-02. Washington, DC: Center for Studying Disability Policy, April 2011.

Stapleton, David C., Bonnie L. O'Day, Gina A. Livermore, and Andrew J. Imparato. "Dismantling the Poverty Trap: Disability Policy for the 21st Century." *The Milbank Quarterly*, vol. 84, no. 4, 2006, pp. 701–732.

Stapleton, David C., Richard V. Burkhauser, Peiyun She, Robert Weathers, and Gina A. Livermore. "Income Security for Workers: A Stressed Support System in Need of Innovation." *Journal of Disability Policy Studies*, vol. 19, no. 4, 2009, pp. 204–220.

Von Wachter, T., J. Song, and J. Manchester. "Trends in Employment and Earnings of Allowed and Rejected Applicants to the Social Security Disability Insurance Program." *American Economic Review*, vol. 101, no. 7, 2011, pp. 3308–3329.

INDEX

#

A

B

H

I

J

L

M

N

O

P

T

U

V

W

Y